R. D. MILLER

INTERPRETING SCHILLER

A STUDY OF FOUR PLAYS

THE DUCHY PRESS

EIGHT LANCASTER ROAD, HARROGATE

MCMLXXXVI

BRITISH LIBRARY CATALOGUING IN PUBLICATION DATA

Interpreting Schiller: Studies of
four Plays
I. Schiller, Friedrich - Criticism and
Interpretation
I. Title
832'.6   PT4292

ISBN 0-9511256-0-5

PRINTED IN GREAT BRITAIN
by WM. HARRISON & SON (RIPON) LIMITED

CONTENTS

CHAPTER ONE

WILHELM TELL

There is in this play a certain underlying tension between two ideals. The curtain rises to the peaceful call of Alpine cowherds and the "harmonious" tinkling of cow-bells, and there is a similar peaceful atmosphere at the end of the play. This tranquil mood reflects the ideal of peace and harmony which is the basis of the moral and religious faith of the Swiss people. Here it is appropriate to refer to the idea of the "idyllic", which Schiller explains as follows. "Der Begriff dieser Idylle ist der Begriff eines völlig aufgelösten Kampfes sowohl in dem einzelnen Menschen, als in der Gesellschaft, einer freien Vereinigung der Neigungen mit dem Gesetze, einer zur höchsten sittlichen Würde hinaufgeläuterten Natur..." (NA.20.472).

"The idea of the idyll, whether in the individual or in society, is that of a struggle which has been completely resolved, the inclinations and the law freely agreeing with each other, Nature purified and raised to the highest moral Dignity."

On the other hand the existence of the oppressive Austrian régime makes it imperative that the Swiss should fight to restore the liberty of the nation. Inevitably a war of liberation involves the use of force, which would run counter to the ideal of peace and harmony. Thus the Swiss are confronted by a dilemma, and it is the tension between the ideal of peace and that of freedom, which forms the main theme of the play. The warnings that are heard, particularly at the Rütli meeting, against lack of moderation in the use of force, reflect Schiller's reaction against the excesses of the French Revolution.

The dilemma is already brought out in 1.2., where Stauffacher's wife Gertrud urges him to consult his friends in the other cantons about the desirability of forming a resistance movement against their Austrian oppressors, on the principle that "injustice, to a noble heart, is unendurable" ("Unbilliges erträgt kein edles Herz", 317). Stauffacher is disturbed to hear his wife summoning discord and the clamour of arms into their peaceful valley (301f.); but as Gertrud sees the matter, it is necessary to use force in defence of liberty. God, it is true, will help the innocent ("Die Unschuld hat im Himmel einen Freund!",324); yet God will be all the more willing to help if men are prepared to fight for their own liberty. Gertrud's assertion that "God helps the courageous" ("Dem Mutigen hilft Gott!",313) is the first of a number of references made from time to time by different characters, both to the help given to man by God and to the self-help to which men resort when they employ force against their oppressors. If the reference is restricted to the help which comes from God, this tends to indicate that the speaker deprecates the use of force and seeks above all to preserve peace; if the emphasis is on self-help, or self-help reinforced by help provided by God, this suggests that the speaker believes in the use of force and cherishes above all the ideal of liberty. The Swiss must either endure oppression in the hope that God will restore their liberty and vindicate His moral order, or else they must themselves attempt to end the oppression, and by doing so run the risk of adding to the prevailing disharmony by the use of force.

In the debate between Tell and Stauffacher in 1.3., the latter is dismayed to find that Tell is inclined to hold himself aloof; but it is not simply his individualism that causes Tell to absent himself from the meeting in the Rütli.

When he is shown the fortress that is being
built at Altdorf, and his attention is drawn to
the dungeons that have been provided to house
anyone inclined to resist the Austrian rule, he
refuses to be unduly disturbed. To the stonema-
son the strength of the walls and buttresses
suggests that they have been built for eternity,
but to Tell, as he gazes from the fortress to
the mountains beyond, the transitory work of human hands is to be contrasted with the truly
eternal world created by God, a world not of
oppression, but of freedom.
　　Was Hände bauten, können Hände stürzen.
　　　　　(nach den Bergen zeigend)
　　Das Haus der Freiheit hat uns Gott
　　　　　　gegründet. (387f.)
The suggestion seems to be that God can be relied upon to preserve the "house of freedom"
which He has established, and that human action
in defence of freedom is unnecessary. Tell's
philosophy of dependence on God is again brought
out when he tells Stauffacher that the only action called for is patience and silence ("Die
einz'ge Tat ist jetzt Geduld und Schweigen",
420). He goes on to describe the oppressive Austrian rule in terms of the storm known as the
"Föhn", which causes ships to seek the protection of the harbour, but which passes harmlessly
over the earth, so long as people remain peacefully at home. Tell implies that such evils as
arise in human affairs will be corrected in the
world created by God. When he adds that "peace
is gladly granted to a peaceful man" –
　　Dem Friedlichen gewährt man gern den Frieden.
– he really gives the true reason for refusing
to attend the Rütli meeting: his desire to keep
the peace, to avoid the use of force. Tell's
good deeds (rescuing Baumgarten, saving a lost
lamb) have not involved taking up arms against
the enemy. He fears that the Rütli meeting will
lead to the use of force and bloodshed, and he

believes that in a world created by God there
should be no need to resort to force. Peace is
therefore the ideal which comes first. He is a
man of peace, a pacifist.

The reason which he gives Stauffacher for
staying away from the meeting - that he cannot
bring himself to spend a long time in deliberation (443) - is merely the excuse which he employs because he does not wish to emphasise the
real point of disagreement, the fact that he
deprecates the use of force which his friend advocates. He shows later, in the monologue, that
he is capable of profound deliberation.

In studying 1.4., where we witness the distress suffered by Melchthal on hearing of the
blinding of his father by the Landvogt Landenberg, we should bear in mind the attempt of a
certain type of anti-idealist writer to argue
that the Rütli meeting is discredited by the
presence of Baumgarten and Melchthal. The theory
seems to be that these two victims of oppression
cannot be genuinely concerned to assist the
cause of national liberation, because they are
obsessed by a desire to avenge themselves in
a private matter. The killing of Wolfenschießen
has been criticised as an act of revenge; but
the text shows that Baumgarten acted, not to
avenge the deed, but to prevent Wolfenschießen
from making the attempt on his wife's honour
(85f.). Even a moderate man like Walther Fürst
expresses his approval of Baumgarten's action,
which to him represents a judgement of God on
Wolfenschießen (552). Baumgarten's patriotism
appears if anything to be heightened by his experience of Austrian oppression; for he is one
of those who later in V.1. (2936f.) express
their determination to resist any attempt by
Austria to re-establish her power in the land.

As for Melchthal, in view of the atrocity
committed against his father it is understanda-
ble that he should at first declare that all his

thoughts will be concentrated on "bloody retali-
ation" (6I6-7). If a mature man like Walther
Fürst has difficulty in mastering his sense of
outrage, it is not surprising that an impetuous
youth should scarcely be able to control himself (483f.). The assertion that the Rütli meeting is discredited by the presence of Melchthal
is demolished by reference to the fact that it
is mainly as a result of the pressure which he
puts upon Walther Fürst and Stauffacher in 1.4.
that the arrangements to hold the meeting are
made in the first place. When Walther Fürst hesitates and prevaricates by suggesting that they
should obtain the opinion of the nobility, particularly Attinghausen, Melchthal sweeps his
evasiveness aside (687-695). So the decision is
made by Walther Fürst, and if it is he who un-
dertakes to recruit supporters in Uri, and Stauffacher is to do likewise in Schwytz, it is Melchthal who is dispatched to Unterwalden to carry
out the same duty there. The atrocity to which
his father has been subjected, far from causing
him to think only of his own troubles, fills him
with a burning zeal to start a national movement
of liberation. So Melchthal is a respected mem-
ber of the group of three men who, at the end of
the scene, solemnly join hands in pledge that
they will stand together, and that the three
cantons will cooperate in the new movement of
national liberation. Moreover, the first part of
2.2. contains further evidence of the enthusiasm
with which Melchthal devotes himself to the national cause, as he relates how he has visited
one Alpine cottage after another, enlisting the
support of the peasants. He also reports with
pride how he has reconnoitred the fortresses of
Roßberg and Sarnen, while refraining from taking
precipitate action.

In studying Act 2, Scene 2, where the Swiss
patriots gather secretly in the Rütli meadow to
work out a plan of campaign to overthrow the

Austrian régime, we must take into consideration
the assertion that these selfsame Swiss patriots, whose aim is to regain their liberty as a
nation, actually contrive in the course of the
meeting to "repudiate bloodshed". How a nation
can set out to regain their liberty by means of
a military campaign, and yet at the same time
"repudiate bloodshed", is not explained.

In truth there are but three men who are
either opposed to the use of force, or who have
reservations about it. They tend to stand out
from the majority of the confederates at the
meeting, who are in favour of the use of force
to restore the liberty of their country. One by
one Rösselmann the parson, Reding the Speaker,
and Walther Fürst urge the confederates either
to renounce the use of force and to negotiate a
peaceful conclusion to the dispute with Austria,
or else counsel caution and moderation in the
use of force. One by one they suffer a rebuff at
the hands of the confederates; the advice they
give is either rejected or discredited.

Stauffacher by his eloquence appeals very
forcefully to the patriotism of his audience,
giving them an account of their past history, in
which they have always been prepared to fight
for their liberty and have made the soil their
own by their labour, until in a moving perora-
tion he inspires them with the determination to
put an end to the Austrian oppression. In doing
so he makes two main points. Firstly, when justice is perverted to injustice by man's earthly
rulers, then he must have recourse to divine
justice, to those eternal laws which exist in-
alienably, as though on a transcendental plane.

Wenn der Gedrückte nirgends Recht kann
finden,
Wenn unerträglich wird die Last - greift er
Hinauf getrosten Mutes in den Himmel,
Und holt herunter seine ewgen Rechte,
Die droben hangen unveräußerlich

Und unzerbrechlich wie die Sterne selbst -
                    (1276-81)
The second point made by Stauffacher is the necessity of resorting to force of arms; for when
the civil authority forfeits all right to gov-
ern, the primeval state of nature returns, in
which one man stands confronting another with
the sword in his hand. Stauffacher describes the
sword as the last resort, but it is one which is
indispensable if they are to defend their wives
and children.
Der alte Urstand der Natur kehrt wieder,
Wo Mensch dem Menschen gegenüber steht -
Zum letzten Mittel, wenn kein andres mehr
Verfangen will, ist ihm das Schwert gegeben
........Wir stehn vor unser Land,
Wir stehn vor unsre Weiber, unsre Kinder!
                    (1282-88)
We see therefore that Stauffacher, in declaring
that the confederates should rely, not only on
divine justice and the help that God will give
them, but also on their own valour, is virtually
echoing Gertrud's aphorism, "Dem Mutigen hilft
Gott!" (312), which might be loosely translated
as "God helps those who help themselves!". In an
earlier scene Walther Fürst expressed the same
idea when he said that God must help the confederates through their own arm ("So muß Gott uns
helfen/Durch unsern Arm", 704f.); though he is
more averse to the use of force than Stauffacher
is at this time.
     The confederates, thoroughly roused by the
speech, repeat Stauffacher's words, "Wir stehn
vor unsre Weiber, unsre Kinder!" (1289) as a
kind of battle-cry, and strike their swords in
a demonstration of martial zeal.
     At this point Rösselmann, one of the three
men of peace at the meeting, intervenes to appeal to the confederates to consider the matter
well, before they take to the sword: he urges
that they should make peace with Austria by

transferring their allegiance from the Empire to
Austria (1295). This causes a violent reaction,
and Reding the Speaker is obliged to accept a
resolution that anyone who advocates submission
to Austria should be deprived of all rights and
honour. Rösselmann, realising that he has been
unwise to go so far as to cause a reaction,
makes a show of welcoming this resolution as a
sign of the confederates' dedication to the
cause of freedom (1311). Another interpretation
(W.F.M.,113f.) is that Rösselmann has made the
suggestion in order to provoke the confederates
to "proclaim unanimity in their common principle". If this is so, one can only wonder why he
should choose this particular moment at which to
unite them, when they have already been united
by Stauffacher's oratory. The answer seems to be
that his true purpose is to moderate the martial
zeal with which Stauffacher has inspired them.

Now Reding, the second of the three men of
peace, addresses the confederates. It was only
"after a pause" that he, as the Speaker, was
able to bring himself to accept the resolution
against submission to Austria (1310): he had to
bow to the will of the majority. He too, like
Rösselmann, appeals to the confederates to consider the matter well, before they commit themselves to the use of force. "Have all the non-
violent methods been attempted?" he asks (1315).
Before the confederates take up the sword, they
should first make sure that their complaint is
brought to the attention of the King of Austria
himself. Next comes a passage which,however familiar it may be through frequent quotation, does
not appear to have been properly understood.

> Schrecklich immer
> Auch in gerechter Sache ist Gewalt,
> Gott hilft nur dann, wenn Menschen nicht
> mehr helfen. (1320-2)

This passage, to which commentators are inclined
to appeal in support of their contention that

"the confederates repudiate bloodshed", gives
expression to the view of one man, though the
two other men of peace probably agree with him.

As we have already seen, belief in the use
of force, combined with help provided by God, is
an important theme in the play. It is exemplified by Gertrud's remark, "Dem Mutigen hilft
Gott!" (313), as well as by Walther Fürst's belief that God must help the confederates through
their own arm (704f.). One commentator, having
quoted those two passages, then goes on to quote
Reding's pronouncement, "Gott hilft nur dann,
wenn Menschen nicht mehr helfen", as though this
last passage were in agreement with the other
two. Yet in the statements by Gertrud and Walther Fürst the use of force by men in fighting
for liberty is associated positively with the
help that God provides. Reding on the other hand
dissociates the use of force from the help that
is given to man by God. God, he says, "helps
only when men no longer help". The reference to
"help" given by men is of course a reference to
force employed by men, the kind of force which
Reding has just described as "terrible even in
a just cause". This does not mean: "Although
force must be accepted in the interest of a good
cause, it must be restricted to a minimum". On
the contrary, it is Reding's belief that even in
a good cause the use of force is unjustified.
The task of restoring freedom to God's world
should be left to God; men should not meddle
with a problem which they might only aggravate.
Thus Reding's declaration directly contradicts
Stauffacher's reference to the return of the
primeval state of nature in which man is per-
mitted, as a last resort, to make use of his
sword (1284f.); it is also opposed to Walther
Fürst's earlier assertion that God must help the
confederates through their own arm (704f.). In
other words Reding, like Tell, is a pacifist,
and his statement that only when men avoid the

use of force will God restore their liberty,
is completely in agreement with Tell's belief
that "the house of freedom has been established
by God" -
Das Haus der Freiheit hat uns Gott gegründet.
                                        (388)
- the implication of which is that God, without
human help, will ensure that His "house of freedom" is preserved.

Reding, in expressing his own view, is very
much in a minority. Indeed, just as Rösselmann
has received a severe rebuff for suggesting that
the Swiss should make peace with Austria, so
Reding's contribution to the debate is rejected
when Konrad Hunn gives a factual account of an
unsuccessful attempt that has already been made
to appeal to the King of Austria to confirm the
ancient liberties of Switzerland. The advice
given to him on that occasion during his visit
to Austria, that the Swiss should "help themselves" and not expect justice from the king,
contradicts Reding's contention that it might
yet be possible to reach an agreement with the
Austrian king. The words "Helft euch selbst!"
("Help yourselves!"), an appeal that the Swiss
people should themselves make their own attempt
to throw off the Austrian oppression, becomes a
battle-cry on the lips of Auf der Mauer (1350).

To Walther Fürst it is a battle-cry which
has overtones of extremism involving the unres-
trained use of violence, and just as Rösselmann
and Reding have already intervened to restrain
the confederates from committing themselves
overhastily to the use of force, so now Walther
Fürst issues a warning against the danger of
extremism in demanding new rights.
Die alten Rechte, wie wir sie ererbt
Von unsern Vätern, wollen wir bewahren,
Nicht ungezügelt nach dem Neuen greifen.
                                    (1354f.)
Whereas in Reding's opinion men should refrain

from using force altogether, and leave God to
restore the freedom that has been lost, Walther
Fürst resigns himself to the necessity of using
a limited degree of force, which will include
the expulsion of the Governors and the destruction of the fortresses, though he hopes somewhat
vainly that this may be done without bloodshed.
 Die Vögte wollen wir mit ihren Knechten
 Verjagen und die festen Schlösser brechen,
 Doch wenn es sein mag, ohne Blut. (1367f.)
This rather pathetic hope that somehow bloodshed
might be avoided in a war of liberation, brings
out very clearly the dilemma in which the moder-
ates find themselves; and just as Rösselmann and
Reding have met with nothing but hostility for
their pains in advocating peace with Austria, so
the advice which Walther Fürst gives tends to be
discredited by the disagreement between his not
very realistic views and those of Reding, who
challenges him to explain how force can be employed without bloodshed. "But tell us! How can
we manage it? The enemy is armed with weapons,
and he will certainly not give way peacefully."
 Doch lasset hören! Wie vollenden wir's?
 Es hat der Feind die Waffen in der Hand,
 Und nicht fürwahr in Frieden wird er
                   weichen. (1376f.)
Reding's purpose is not to suggest that the confederates should resign themselves to the bloodshed that is inseparable from the use of force,
but to warn Walther Fürst against committing
himself to the use of force on the false assumption that bloodshed can be avoided.
    The proposal that the action that is con-
templated against the Austrian rulers should be
postponed, a proposal which is accepted by 20 to
12, is not the work of the small peace party. It
is put forward by Winkelried, a true patriot who
listens entranced to Stauffacher's account of
the past history of the Swiss people (1162f.),
and who is quick to denounce Rösselmann as a

traitor for suggesting that the Swiss people should swear allegiance to Austria (1297). The advantage of the postponement (as explained by Winkelried, 1400f.) is the prospect offered by the Christmas festival of a favourable opportunity for gaining admittance to the fortresses of Sarnen and Roßberg, as well as the possibility of smuggling in weapons under cover of taking presents to the Governor (1405f.). This last feature of the plan scarcely suggests that the liberation of the nation will be effected without bloodshed.

Stauffacher expresses his concern about the resistance which Geßler must be expected to offer to any attempt by the confederates to regain their liberty; in view of the fact that he would not yield without bloodshed, Stauffacher believes that it would be unwise to spare his life.

Nicht ohne Blut räumt er das Feld, ja selbst
Vertrieben bleibt er furchtbar noch dem Land,
Schwer ists und fast gefährlich, ihn zu
        schonen. (1430-2)

Although Baumgarten offers to undertake the hazardous task of dispatching Geßler, declaring that he will gladly risk his life for the sake of his country (1433f.), Reding manages to prevent any further discussion of the subject. The sight of the dawn reaching the mountain-tops (an image which in general in Schiller's works represents the first blush of Beauty heralding, it may be, the reign of Reason) inspires the confederates to take a solemn oath, dedicating themselves to the cause of Liberty.

Wir wollen frei sein wie die Väter waren,
Eher den Tod, als in der Knechtschaft leben.
        (1450)

But Reding the pacifist, reacting against Stauffacher's proposal that they should commit themselves to bloodshed in the case of Geßler, uses the dawn as an excuse to draw the meeting to a

close, on the ground that the daylight might reveal their secret meeting to their oppressors
(1441f.). Walther Fürst, however, points out
that there is no need for anxiety on that score,
because as he says "night departs slowly from
the valleys" (1443).

The conclusion to be reached from our study
of the Rütli meeting is that there is no justification for the claim that the confederates are
so foolish as to "repudiate bloodshed" at the
very time when they intend to use force in an
attempt to regain their liberty. They demonstrate their determination to fight for liberty
by their enthusiastic response to Stauffacher's
speech, by their fierce opposition to Rösselmann's appeal that they should swear allegiance
to Austria, by Stauffacher's insistence that
Geßler must be put to death, and by the oath
that they swear to fight and if necessary to
die, rather than live in servitude. Even though
the confederates would agree that the use of
force is terrible even in a just cause, they
still believe that it is necessary: they do not
share Reding's belief that "God helps only when
men no longer help".

As we have seen, the thesis that Baumgarten
and Melchthal become so obsessed with their need
to avenge the wrong which each of them has sustained that they lose sight of the national interest, is not based on the evidence of the text.
Indeed as the play progresses the evidence of
their patriotism accumulates still further. We
have seen that Baumgarten offers to undertake
the hazardous task of dispatching Geßler. Melchthal offers to play the leading part in capturing the fortress of Roßberg, by scaling the wall
with a rope-ladder, before admitting the other
confederates engaged in the operation (1413ff.).
Later we hear that he not only successfully fulfils this task (2875), but also that he and Rudenz rescue Bertha from the flames (2893f.).

If anti-idealist commentators, attempting
to discredit such patriotic characters as Baumgarten and Melchthal, have paid scarcely any
attention to the evidence of the text, their
attempts to disparage Tell have been even more
at variance with the text. In the scene where he
is ordered to shoot at an apple placed on his
his son's head, he is accused of grovelling before Geßler. But what are the facts? When Tell
is threatened with arrest for failing to show
respect to Geßler's hat, some of his friends
attempt to rescue him, and it is the commotion
they cause which brings Geßler on the scene.
Tell, aware of what is at stake - the life of
his son and those of his countrymen who are
present - counsels caution (1846) and addresses
Geßler respectfully (1870). He is not the only
person who shows restraint: his father-in-law
Walther Fürst even goes down on his knees, be-
seeching Geßler to show mercy (1943ff.). The
reason for such restraint is clear: the Swiss
are without weapons, and they are surrounded by
what Stauffacher calls a "forest of lances".
    Es ist umsonst. Wir haben keine Waffen,
    Ihr seht den Wald von Lanzen um uns her.
                                        (1968)
It is no part of a patriot's duty to endanger
the lives of his compatriots. The incident also
shows how important it is that the confederates
should be able to use force to defend themselves
against their oppressors.
    But the gravest charge brought against Tell
is that he deliberately endangers his son's life
in order to demonstrate his skill as a marksman.
If this were true, it would turn the hero of the
play into a monster; but it is a charge which
can be sustained only by turning a blind eye to
the text. In the first place Tell is told that
he is to shoot at an apple placed on his son's
head, and that if he fails to hit the apple, his
life will be forfeit.

Denn fehlst du ihn, so ist dein Kopf verloren.
(1889)
When Tell replies that he would rather die than
put his son's life at risk, Geßler retorts: "You
will shoot or you will die together with your
boy."
Du schießest oder stirbst mit deinem Knaben.
(1899)
If Tell had refused to undertake what was
demanded of him, the death of his son (and his
own death) would have followed inevitably. In
complying with the order, he takes the course
that offers some possibility that his son's life
will be saved. The anti-idealist commentator has
no words with which to condemn the inhumanity of
Geßler in mocking the pure feelings that exist
in a father's heart. It is the "inhumanity" of
Tell, in rescuing his son from the threat of
death at Geßler's hands, that he condemns. It is
no excuse to point out that Tell's wife herself
blames him for endangering the life of his son.
She was not present at the ordeal undergone by
her husband, and is ignorant of the circumstances. We as commentators were present, and it is
our privilege to bear witness to the truth.
If Tell has been undeservedly blamed for
caring more for his reputation as a marksman
than for his son's life, he has also been inap-
propriately praised by another commentator who
attributes to him a motive which cannot truly be
laid at his door. We are told that he decides to
obey Geßler, not in the hope that he will succeed in saving his son's life, but in the per-
verse belief that it is right to defer to the
legitimate civil authorities, no matter how mon-
strously unjust they may be. It seems that this
"sublime" decision overrules, not only his concern for his son, but also his faith in a moral
order presided over by God, an order flouted by
Geßler. Both of these misinterpretations are at
variance with the evidence of the text; for if

Tell cares less for his son's life than he does
for demonstrating either his skill as a marksman
or his obedience to the civil authority, why in
the first place does he refuse to shoot? Why
does he agree to shoot only when Geßler warns
him that if he continues to refuse, his son's
life as well as his own will be forfeited?

Again, Tell is castigated for abandoning
the ship entrusted to him in the storm. He did
not go on board as a navigator, but as a prison-
er; and yet we are asked to believe that it is
his duty to steer the ship safely through the
storm, in order that Geßler may incarcerate him
in a dungeon where neither moon nor sun will
shine upon him (2066f.), thus enabling Geßler to
continue his oppressive rule and denying his
fellow countrymen the help that he, Tell, might
otherwise have given them.

When Rudenz witnesses the inhumanity of
Geßler in ordering Tell to shoot in circumstances which endanger his son's life, he speaks of
the scales falling from his eyes (2016), i.e. he
becomes convinced of the serious error he has
made in siding with the Austrians against his
own people. Tell himself undergoes a conversion
too. His heart has always been in sympathy with
his fellow countrymen; but as a result of the
terrible ordeal which he has undergone, he now
becomes convinced that it is not enough to rely
on God to put an end to the oppression and to
set men free; for it is through the deeds of man
that God works His will in the world. In other
words Tell renounces his pacifism, which kept
him away from the Rütli meeting, and prepares to
attack the evil system by striking down its most
evil embodiment, Geßler.

In his monologue in 4.3. Tell dwells on the
quiet peaceful life he has led, thus reminding
us of the pacifism that caused him to absent
himself from the Rütli meeting.

Ich lebte still und harmlos - Das Geschoß

War auf des Waldes Tiere nur gerichtet,
Meine Gedanken waren rein von Mord-(2568-70)
Even now, when the "milk of his pious disposition" has been converted by Geßler's inhumanity
to "seething dragon's venom" (2572f.), by discussing the revulsion that he feels, he achieves
a certain freedom from it. The profoundly medi-
tative, deliberative mood of the monologue makes
it clear that the deed which he is contemplating
will be carried out on principle, not on impulse. Tell is now opposed to the view advanced
by Reding that "God helps when men no longer
help" (1322), as well as to his own previous belief that God Himself, without human assistance,
will preserve the "house of freedom" that he has
established (388). Tell's creed is now identical
with that propounded by Stauffacher at the Rütli
meeting, when in 11.1275-88 he declared that if
justice is perverted to injustice by men's
earthly rulers, they must have recourse to divine justice, and in the last resort, in order
to defend their wives and children, take up the
sword. So Tell in 11.2590-6 of his monologue (as
though to refute the assertion of certain commentators that he fails to mention the political
aspect of the matter) declares that Geßler, although he is legally his master and the Emper-
or's appointed Governor, has forfeited all moral
authority on account of the acts of inhumanity
which he has perpetrated. Tell implies that if
those who by the authority they exercise have a
duty to uphold the moral order, actually violate
that order by their injustice and inhumanity,
then God will exact punishment and retribution.
Du bist mein Herr und meines Kaisers Vogt,
Doch nicht der Kaiser hätte sich erlaubt
Was du - Er sandte dich in diese Lande,
Um Recht zu sprechen - strenges, denn er
                              zürnet -
Doch nicht um mit der mörderischen Lust
Dich jedes Greuels straflos zu erfrechen,

Es lebt ein Gott zu strafen und zu rächen.

It is Tell who is to exact retribution on behalf of God. Just as Stauffacher at the end of the speech to which we have referred appeals to the confederates to take up the sword and to stand ready to defend their wives and children, so Tell prepares to protect his innocent children and his faithful wife from Geßler's inhumanity.

Die armen Kindlein, die unschuldigen,
Das treue Weib muß ich vor deiner Wut
Beschützen, Landvogt... (2577ff.)

Anti-idealists in their comments on the monologue sometimes make a false distinction be- "private" and "political" motives, and then pro- ceed to argue that Tell kills Geßler mainly for "private" reasons, which it is implied are less valid than political reasons. Stauffacher in his speech appeals to the confederates to take up arms, both to destroy an evil political system and to protect their families. So Tell in his monologue prepares to kill Geßler both as the embodiment of that evil political system and as a monster who threatens his family. In Tell's case as in the cases of the other confederates the safety of their families is their most imme- diate concern, but it is very much bound up with the need to liberate the country as a whole. The "political" and "private" aspects of the libera- tion movement are united by the concept of the moral order to which both are related. When Geß- ler required Tell to shoot so as to endanger his own son, he violated the moral order, thus caus- ing Tell to swear an oath "which only God could hear", that Geßler must no longer be allowed to live; it is an oath which Tell considers a "sac- red obligation" which he must fulfil.

Damals gelobt' ich mir in meinem Innern
Mit furchtbarm Eidschwur, den nur Gott
                              gehört,
Daß meines nächsten Schusses erstes Ziel
Dein Herz sein sollte - Was ich mir gelobt

In jenes Augenblickes Höllenqualen,
Ist eine heilge Schuld, ich will sie zahlen.
                    (2584ff.)
When Geßler, appointed to his position in order
that he may rule justly ("um Recht zu sprechen",
2593), neglects that duty in order to commit
every conceivable atrocity, he cannot escape the
punishment and retribution meted out to him by
God (2596). Comparing these two aspects of the
judgement of Geßler, must we say that the first
is merely "private", simply because Tell's family is involved, and that only the second is
"political"? Geßler's failure to rule justly,
and the offences he commits against individual
members of the community, are one and the same
offence against the moral order. Tell, in defending his family, is at the same time acting
on behalf of the moral order.

     In his representation of the actual shoot-
ing of Geßler, Schiller takes great pains to
portray him, not simply as the enemy of Tell and
his family, but as a public enemy, a tyrant who
threatens the freedom and happiness of the whole
Swiss people. His inhumanity is demonstrated by
his refusal to listen to the woman Armgart, who
complains that her husband has been imprisoned
for six months without a trial, and who lies
down in Geßler's path in an attempt to make him
stop and listen to her. To argue that Tell cannot have been influenced in his decision to kill
Geßler by the pity that he feels for the woman,
since he has made his decision before the woman
appears, is a mere quibble. The point is that
Schiller, by introducing this episode, is illus-
trating the kind of injustice of which Tell is
already well aware, and is also reminding the
spectator or the reader that Tell, in killing
Geßler, is not simply acting in his own private
affair. Finally, as Tell's arrow strikes home,
Geßler is promising to take still sterner measures, in order to "break the impudent spirit of
freedom".

Den kecken Geist der Freiheit will ich
                    beugen. (2783)
In these circumstances it is clear that Tell's
act is justified not only by his desire to protect his family, but as an act of national liberation. The latter aspect is stressed when Tell
declares that "the cottages are free, and innocence is no longer endangered" by Geßler; nor is
he any longer a danger to the nation as a whole.
Frei sind die Hütten, sicher ist die Unschuld
Vor dir, du wirst dem Lande nicht mehr
                    schaden. (2793f.)
Commentators sometimes pass over this passage in
silence, or else they pretend that it is only in
the second place, as a kind of after-thought,
that Tell refers to his "political" motive. But
we have already pointed out that Tell's acceptance of the political aims of men like Stauffacher is an integral part of his monologue and
is made particularly clear in 11.2590-6. It is
a moral as well as a political motive, an appeal
to the same moral order as that invoked by Stauffacher in 11.1275-88.

In 4.1. Tell sends a message to his wife to
inform her of his escape from Geßler (2290ff.);
then, having discharged his "private" duty, he
proceeds to fulfil his "political" obligation by
sending a similar message to those who attended
the Rütli meeting, informing them that he is
free and that they will soon hear more of him
(2294-8). This is another indication that Tell
does not consider the killing of Geßler simply
as a private affair.

But we have seen that after "all" the confederates had rallied to Stauffacher's appeal,
acclaiming the moral order which he invoked, and
vowing to defend their wives and children with
the sword, they then voted by 20 against 12 in
favour of postponing the intended action against
their oppressors. We have seen that this was not
a decision in favour of pacifism. The proposal

was put forward by Winkelried, not by one of the
pacifists, Reding, Rösselmann or Walther Fürst.
It included a plan for capturing the fortresses
and for the use of weapons in doing so. Had it
not been for these features of the proposal, had
it been merely a peace proposal, it would not
have been accepted; it would have met with the
same hostile reception as Rösselmann's earlier
peace proposal; it would have been rejected as
decisively as Reding's argument was demolished
by Konrad Hunn.

But although Winkelried's motion was not
seen as a pacifist motion by the confederates
who voted on it, although Stauffacher (after the
adoption of the motion) urged the necessity of
killing Geßler, and the meeting ended with the
oath by which the confederates swore to die if
necessary in defence of their liberty - nevertheless, by bringing about a delay in the use of
force in defence of liberty, it does in fact, in
the short term, play into the hands of Geßler.
As the latter orders Tell to shoot at his own
son, Melchthal, watching helplessly, challenges
his fellow countrymen with the question, "Wozu
haben wir geschworen?" (1967). He directly con-
nects the ordeal which Tell is undergoing with
the vote in favour of delaying action against
the oppressors.

Verzeihs Gott denen, die zum Aufschub rieten!
(1971)

Rudenz too regards the ordeal to which Tell is
subjected as resulting from the failure of the
confederates to take action (2510ff.).

But after the men of Rütli have postponed
taking action against their oppressors, their
failure, as though providentially, corrects itself. It is corrected partly by Tell and partly
by Melchthal and Rudenz acting under the pressure of subsequent events. The ordeal which Tell
undergoes gives him a new insight into the depth
of Geßler's inhumanity, and impels him to rid

the world of such a monster. So Tell, having overcome his pacifism by the understanding which he has gained of the radical nature of the evil that is present in Geßler, is able to make his own contribution by undertaking the task which Baumgarten offered to carry out, that of killing Geßler. The fact that this task fulfilled by Tell was originally proposed by Stauffacher as an undertaking that was necessary purely in the national interest, is yet another indication of its "political" nature.

Tell's action against Geßler, and that of Rudenz and Melchthal in capturing the fortresses are not coordinated, but they both arise from a reaction (a) against Geßler's inhumanity toward Tell, and (b) either against the Rütli decision in favour of delay, or in Tell's case against his own pacifism. The killing of Geßler is not to be seen as an isolated act without any effect on the war of liberation in general. Rudolph der Harras notes that the people at once react to the death of Geßler by throwing off their fear and what he calls their "obedience" (2822), and he realises that as a result of the blow struck by Tell, the fortresses are endangered (2827).

In view of the treatment meted out to Tell, Melchthal considers that he has been freed from his obligation to abide by the decision taken at the Rütli meeting to postpone action (2549ff.). Rudenz, who was not present at the meeting, announces his intention of taking independent action against the Austrians. Melchthal accepts Rudenz as his leader (2547); and before long the latter is giving orders to Stauffacher and Walther Fürst, instructing them that while he and Melchthal see to the attack on the fortresses, they are to arm themselves and await the signal for the uprising (2553f.).

Yet even when the beacons have been lit on the mountains, announcing that the fortresses have been taken and that the uprising is to

begin, there is no evidence that either Walther
Fürst or Stauffacher gives orders for the attack
to be started; apparently they consider themselves bound by the decision taken at the Rütli
meeting. The people, left to themselves, take
matters into their own hands and begin to pull
down the local fortress; Walther Fürst actually
attempts to dissuade them, but seeing the futility of his attempt, soon gives up (2864). Yet
despite his aversion to the use of force, he is
eager enough, when Melchthal arrives, to hear
the news that freedom has been won and that the
land has been cleared of the enemy (2867f.). He
seeks the goal of liberty, but is not willing to
pay the price by using the force that is necessary to reach that goal. That he leaves to the
combattants. What a remarkable thing it is that
in Melchthal's account of the assault on the
fortress of Roßberg there is not the slightest
mention of any casualties, on either side. It is
all made to sound so easy. "When we had cleared
the castle of the enemy and had joyfully set
fire to it..."

Als wir das Schloß
Vom Feind geleert, nun freudig angezündet...
(2876f.)

In Act 5 (as well as in the scene in the Rütli)
the confederates are armed with swords, battle-
axes and spiked clubs (H.K.181), and as Reding
pointed out, it is scarcely credible that armed
soldiers would give way without offering resistance (1379). Bloodshed there must have been; yet
neither Walther Fürst nor Melchthal attempts to
discuss the matter. We hear that Bertha's life
is endangered by the fire that has been started,
but happily she is rescued. Walther Fürst, hearing that the life of Landenberg, who blinded
Melchthal's father, has been spared, declares:
"It is well for you that you have not desecrated
the pure victory with bloodshed!".

Wohl euch, daß ihr den reinen Sieg
Mit Blute nicht geschändet! (2912f.).

As for the bloodshed that must have occurred during the attack on Sarnen and Roßberg, a veil is drawn over that.

We come now to the Parricida episode. The letter written by Schiller to Iffland (H.K.179) confirms the rôle played by this character in setting off Tell's sterling qualities with his own criminal propensity. "Over against the infamous murder motivated by impiety and ambition stands Tell's necessary deed, which appears guiltless in comparison with such a dissimilar case; and the main idea of the whole play is thus stated: the necessity and justice of self-defence in a strictly defined case" ("Das Notwendige und Rechtliche der Selbsthilfe in einem streng bestimmten Fall").

Even here, in their comments on this letter, the anti-idealists attempt to keep up a desperate rearguard action. Schiller does not say, as is alleged, that the killing of Geßler appears guiltless "only" in comparison with the murder committed by Parricida: he says that the Parricida episode in itself suffices to resolve, both morally and practically, Tell's action in killing Geßler. In a letter to Iffland dated 14th April 1804 (Jonas VII, 138) he stresses the importance not only of the Parricida episode, but also of Tell's monologue, in justifying the assassination of Geßler.

A typical example of the confused thought that prevails on the subject of Tell and Parricida is the assertion that Parricida's contribution to the liberty of Switzerland exceeds that of Tell himself, since the Emperor was a greater threat to freedom than was Geßler. Such an assertion is wholly in the spirit of the ridiculous claim made by Parricida himself: "Ich hab das Land von ihm befreit" (3155). It is surely not necessary to point out that Parricida deserves no credit for a wholly fortuitous effect of his atrocious action in murdering the Emperor. Let us suppose that the Emperor, while out hunting, had been thrown by his horse and killed: would we have been told that the horse had freed the land more effectively than Tell? There is not the slightest evidence to suggest that the desire to liberate Switzerland was a contributing factor in motivating Parricida at the time he committed the murder; it is only after the event that he tries to justify his action by appealing to its effect on the situation in Switzerland.

A not less confused reaction to the Parricida episode is the objection that has been raised to the "contradiction" between the confederates' approval of Tell's action in killing Geßler and their condemnation of Parricida's murder of the Emperor. It seems that the confederates' judgement is sounder than that of certain commentators. Tell is concerned to protect his family, he aims to save his country from oppression, he seeks to restore the moral order: Parricida murders his uncle, he acts without thought of others, and the revenge that he takes is out of all proportion to the wrong which he has suffered. How can we fail to see that Tell is justified by his good motives, and that Parricida is condemned by his bad motives?

When Parricida has the effrontery to claim that he has liberated the country, and then persists in trying to put himself on a level with Tell by maintaining that both have avenged themselves on their enemy (3174), Tell bursts out in a wholly justified expostulation, in which he makes clear the absolute distinction between their respective motives.

Darfst du der Ehrsucht blutge Schuld
        vermengen
Mit der gerechten Notwehr eines Vaters?
Hast du der Kinder liebes Haupt verteidigt?
Des Herdes Heiligtum beschützt?...
- Zum Himmel heb' ich meine reinen Hände,
Verfluche dich und deine Tat - Gëracht

Hab ich die heilige Natur, die du
Geschändet... (3175-83)

The commentator who describes Tell's expostulation as "self-righteous" has scarcely any understanding of the meaning of what has taken place
in the play. Is Tell to be deterred from vindi-
cating the leading ideals of this work - the existence of a moral order, the sacredness of the
emotions of pure nature which bind together the
members of a family - lest some critic should
come along and speak uncomprehendingly about
"self-righteousness"? How free from self-righteousness Tell is, how deeply he regrets the need
for bloodshed, he has already shown in his monologue. Tell has looked the evil of the killing
of Geßler in the face, he has taken upon himself
the "guilt" of the deed for the sake of the purpose, the ideals of liberty and pure nature
which transcend it. It is not only Tell's right
but his duty to reprove Parricida for attempting
to put his own selfish, materialistic motives on
a level with Tell's idealistic purposes; had he
failed to do so, he would have been false to
the ideal of freedom for which he and the other
confederates have fought. The means employed,
the use of force, is not forgotten; the tragedy
at the centre of human existence remains. But
when the battle against oppression has been won,
it is right that the triumph of liberty, and of
idealism, should be celebrated.

The murder of the Emperor by Parricida does
not render the Swiss uprising superfluous. Some
commentators make the facile assumption that the
death of the Emperor signifies the end of all
Austrian claims on Switzerland; but when Stauffacher expresses the hope that the new Emperor
will protect Switzerland from Austria's desire
for revenge (3028), he seems to imply that the
danger of some Austrian reaction to the Swiss
uprising has not been altogether removed by the
death of the Emperor.

To speak of Parricida as "freeing" Switzerland betrays a lack of understanding of freedom,
and of what it means to free a nation. The freedom of the Swiss nation, as affirmed by Stauffacher at the Rütli meeting, is rooted in the
whole past history of their land, in the labour
by which they made it theirs, in the jealousy
with which they have always guarded their freedom (even from the Emperor), in the thousand
years during which they have owned the soil.
Their freedom is furthermore sanctioned by the
moral order to which they appeal when the tyran-
ny that has been imposed on them, becomes intol-
erable. This view of freedom is also implicit
in Attinghausen's vision of a nation of shep-
herds gladly sacrificing themselves for the liberty of their land (2438-46). It is a view of
freedom, the freedom of commitment, for which no
substitute can be found in what might be called
external freedom, the work of a mere fortuitous
occurrence, such as the death of the King of
Austria. What purpose would that other freedom
serve, external as opposed to internal freedom,
if the people were not themselves committed to
fighting for their freedom and preserving the
values that they have always held dear?

When Stauffacher, referring to the murder
of the King of Austria, describes the Swiss as
"plucking the precious fruit of the bloody crime
with their pure hand" -
Wir aber brechen mit der reinen Hand
Des blutgen Frevels segenvolle Frucht.(3016f)
- he invests his words with a certain bitter irony, an irony which passes over the heads of
many a critic. It was Stauffacher who at the
Rütli meeting was the champion par excellence of
that true inner freedom of which we have spoken.
Since then the resolution delaying the proposed
action, a resolution which he feels obliged to
abide by, has compelled him to remain inactive
while the cause of liberty is being championed

by Tell, Melchthal and Rudenz. Finally comes the
news of the murder of the King of Austria, an
external factor in the situation. Stauffacher,
far from suggesting that the Swiss should con-
gratulate themselves on a stroke of good luck
which might appear to them to have given them
freedom without their having to fight for it,
directs his irony particularly at those who seek
to safeguard their moral purity by avoiding the
use of force and bloodshed. We are reminded of
the words with which Walther Fürst congratulates
Melchthal on having refrained from desecrat-
ing the "pure" victory by the shedding of blood;
but as we have seen, Walther Fürst deludes himself in thinking that victory can be won without bloodshed (supra 23). Stauffacher, more
clear-sighted than Walther Fürst, would have
liked nothing better than to commit himself to
the cause of liberty by the use of force, even
if it should entail bloodshed.

It is not unusual for a commentator to
criticise the Swiss people in this play for ap-
plying a double standard in judging different
characters; indeed it is a criticism which has
become a kind of cliché with anti-idealist commentators. Let us take two examples of this sort
of comment.

In the first example we are told that a
double standard is applied in praising Melchthal
for his "restraint", and in praising Tell for
his "lack of restraint". It is immediately ap-
parent that it might well be misleading to compare two persons, or to represent the Swiss as
comparing two persons, simply and solely by making one particular quality (restraint or lack of
restraint) the sole criterion in judging them.
It is true that restraint in the use of force
and the avoidance of unnecessary bloodshed is an
important principle with the confederates. But
the main purpose of those who attend the Rütli
meeting is to liberate their country, not simply

to practise the art of restraint. It would not
have made sense if the confederates had judged
Melchthal and Tell merely according to the degree of restraint which they show. Nor in fact
do they do so, as an examination of the text
makes clear. When the commentator refers to the
confederates as praising Melchthal for his restraint, he is presumably referring to the passage in which Walther Fürst congratulates Melchthal on having avoided tarnishing the "pure"
victory by taking revenge on Landenberg (2912).
But Walther Fürst's first concern, when he meets
Melchthal after the fighting, is to enquire, not
whether the victory has been "pure" in the sense
of "free from bloodshed", but whether Melchthal
has in fact helped to restore the liberty of the
land, whether he has so to speak "purged" the
land of the enemy.

Seid ihr es, Melchthal? Bringt ihr uns die
Freiheit?
Sagt! Sind die Lande alle rein vom Feind?
(2867f.)

If we are to take Walther Fürst, in his judgement of Melchthal, as representing the confederates in general, then we must say that they
praise Melchthal, not in the first place because
he has shown restraint in sparing the life of
Landenberg, but because he has made an effective
contribution to the liberation of the country.

So too in the case of Tell, the Swiss people acclaim him, not because he has shown "lack
of restraint", but because he has struck an
effective blow for liberty. This rather obvious
point (the kind of obvious truth which one is
obliged to state in refuting the more peculiar
arguments of the anti-idealists) is made for example by Stüssi.

Wir erdulden
Keine Gewalt mehr. Wir sind freie Menschen.
(2819f.)

It is a point that is unanimously confirmed by

those present at the death of Geßler, and again
in the final scene.

Es lebe Tell! der Schütz und der Erretter!
(3281)

Now let us consider how the two characters
compare in the restraint or lack of restraint
that they show. Restraint is not exactly the
quality which we associate with the impetuous
Melchthal. As he himself points out, it was not
his doing that Landenberg was not blinded, in
revenge for his action in blinding Melchthal's
father.

Nicht lags an mir, daß er das Licht der Augen
Davon trug... (2903)

In fact Melchthal's sword was already poised
over Landenberg ("Geschwungen über ihm war schon
das Schwert", 2907), when the latter was pardoned by Melchthal's father. The sword which
Melchthal holds aloft over his intended victim
reminds us that he is not unpractised in the use
of that weapon, and that he must have used it to
good effect in the fighting and bloodshed which
must have taken place before the fortress of
Roßberg was captured. If we are to accept the
rather strange assumption that in a war against
an oppressive régime the use of force is always
to be condemned as arising from lack of restraint, how can we condone Melchthal's action
in setting fire to the fortress of Roßberg? Our
purpose is not to discredit Melchthal, but simply to reject the attempt to debunk Tell as a
hero, by contrasting him with a false image of
a Melchthal who has shed no blood.

As for Tell, we have already seen that the
thoughtful mood of his monologue itself tends to
dissociate the killing of Geßler from "lack of
restraint". We are told that Tell's main motive
in killing Geßler is his desire for revenge in
a private matter. Three references are given in
support of this argument, but the passages are
not examined. In the first passage (2060ff.)

Tell declares that if his first arrow had struck his son, his second would have been aimed at Geßler. In the second passage (2584ff.), which forms part of the monologue, Tell refers to his decision to kill Geßler; it was a decision which he affirmed in an oath to God, and which he regards as a sacred obligation. In neither of these passages does Tell speak of "revenge", and in the second it is made clear that his decision to kill Geßler is associated with the need to vindicate the moral order presided over by God. The third passage referred to, but not quoted, is again from the monologue (2596).

Es lebt ein Gott zu strafen und zu rächen.

Here, it is true, there is mention of "revenge"; but it is God, not Tell, who is to take revenge, or Tell on behalf of God. So in this passage, as in the second, it is the moral order that is to be vindicated.

Our second example of this false kind of criticism is the charge that the confederates apply a double standard in first repudiating bloodshed at the Rütli meeting, and in subsequently acclaiming Tell for killing Geßler. We have already refuted the thesis that the confederates repudiate bloodshed at that meeting. When Stauffacher urges the necessity of killing Geßler, not a single dissenting voice is heard. Indeed, Baumgarten offers his services in carrying out the suggestion. Reding, not daring to oppose the majority opinion openly, brings the meeting to a close. How then can it be asserted that the confederates are inconsistent when they acclaim Tell for carrying out the deed?

It is evidence of the obtrusiveness of existentialism in modern Schiller criticism, not only that it should be thought fitting to compare Schiller's "Wilhelm Tell" with Sartre's "Les Mouches", but that the critic should, as he says, reread Schiller's play in the light of the existentialist position, even though he admits

that Schiller would have repudiated this reading (L.W.K.13). We are told that an idealist
acts on "absolute and binding standards", which
"by definition bind and circumscribe our freedom" (ibid 7), whereas the deed committed by Orestes in "Les Mouches" "not only lacks the support of common morality but violates every principle of such morality: his deed is murder and
matricide, but - it is his deed" (ibid 8). So we
are presented with the familiar existentialist
belief that moral law is opposed to freedom, and
that immoralism is practically equivalent to
freedom.

Let us take each part of this statement
separately. Firstly we obey a moral law, not in
a spirit of servile obedience, but because as
rational and moral beings, we identify ourselves
with the moral law, so that in acting on it we
feel as though we were acting on our own moral
principle. In fact we are doing so; for although
a man may not have personally created moral law,
he is part of a whole moral and rational order
of men, by whom moral law has collectively been
created.

Secondly it is possible to believe the assertion that Orestes' crime is in a peculiar
sense "his" deed, a deed by which he frees not
only himself, but also the people of Argos from
the "power of an enslaving law" (L.W.K.12), only
if we accept the whole existentialist philosophy
which underlies this belief. Making "existence"
precede "essence", rejecting all principles and
values that have come down to us from the past,
in practice turns out to be a blueprint for immoralism. Orestes says that he can no longer
distinguish Right and Wrong (Théatre.62), and
the critic tells us that according to existentialist dogma we can never do wrong (L.W.K.9);
but if Orestes does not believe in Right, he
needs it as something from which he can "free"
himself by doing Wrong, thereby enjoying the

illusion of being free. To base our action on no
principle, to act in an entirely arbitrary way,
to give oneself up to licence, is the negation
of freedom.

At this point we are told that, although
existentialism rejects everything that is given,
it does not reject principles; existentialist
man acts on his own principles. Orestes himself
says that he is "condemned to have no other law
but his own" (Théatre.101). When critics of existentialism complain that it leads to lawlessness and anarchy, Sartre replies by announcing
that "existentialism is humanism". After declaring that the individual determines his own self
by his free choice of action, he appeals to this
as evidence of man's "dignity" (E.H.22). The man
who determines or chooses his own self, is at
the same time acting as a "legislator" who also
"chooses" the whole of mankind (ibid.28). The
critic maintains that any similarity that this
statement by Sartre bears to Kant's categorical
imperative, is merely superficial; but he himself virtually admits that we set up a standard
of rightness and wrongness by our actions based
on our own decisions (L.W.K.9).

So the existentialist hero is not after all
irresponsible. Indeed, compared with the idealist hero, who simply has to act on a set of
principles handed down from the past, the existentialist hero is a veritable paragon of responsibility, who anxiously makes up his principles for himself. What comfort the idealist de-
rives from his moral order, and "what anguish if
man has to make his decisions solely on his own
responsibility!" (ibid.7).

This contrast that is drawn between idealism and existentialism is illusory. In practice
it is not Orestes the existentialist, but Tell
the idealist who, in that long monologue preceding the shooting of the tyrant, agonises over
his decision. To think of idealism as a "comfortable" philosophy, because it provides you

with a conscience and a set of ready-made principles, is to overlook a number of factors. The
principles are of a general nature, a decision
has to be made whether to apply a certain principle or not, or how to apply it in the given
circumstances. The powers-that-be may well be
opposed to your ideals, as Tell and Posa know to
their cost; or an army of invasion may stand in
the way of the realisation of your ideals, as
Johanna knows to her cost. There is a far from
completely idealistic world to contend with, not
to mention the baser side of your own nature,
your sinfulness.

If the picture of the "comfortable" idealist is illusory, are we more convinced by the
image of the existentialist racked by the lonely
and awful responsibility of decision-making?
Does Orestes undergo any terrifying spells of
existentialist "Angst", do we see him writhing
in Kierkegaardian "fear and trembling"? Well,
hardly. On the whole he quite enjoys his existentialist experience, as freedom comes "crash-
ing down" on him, sweeping him off his feet
(Théatre.101). It is not so much with "Angst" as
with a certain gusto that he looks forward to
his task of destroying the city of Argos and its
two rulers, one of whom is his mother. "I'll
turn into an axe and hew those walls asunder,
ripping open the bellies of those stolid houses,
and there will steam up from the gashes a stench
of rotting food and incense" (ibid.64). Electra
says that she and Orestes will never rest again
until the King and Queen are both lying on their
backs, "with faces like crushed mulberries"
(ibid.66); and as Orestes strikes the King with
his sword, he feels no remorse, because he is
"only doing what is right" (ibid.80).

The method employed by Mathieu in "Les
Chemins de la Liberté" in deciding whether to
take part in the imminent war, throws an inter-
esting sidelight on the torments suffered by the

existentialist hero as he makes his agonising
decision on behalf of all mankind. Accepting the
decision of a tossed coin, he decides to take
part "by pure chance", and is gratified to believe that he is "at the extremest point of
freedom, a martyr without a motive" (C.L.2.218).
Such gratuitous or unmotivated action seems to
be more typical of the existentialist character
than is the responsible decision–making that belongs to existentialist lore.

If nevertheless it is maintained that the
existentialist hero is after all not without
principle, if as we have seen Orestes has no
other law but his own, what exactly is the principle or the law that inspires him? His motive
is not to punish the King and Queen for having
murdered Agamemnon; for he does not believe in
Right and Wrong. Can we say that his law is that
it is good to free oneself from moral law by doing what is wrong without suffering remorse?
That is nearer the mark. But we must remember
Sartre's dictum that when a man acts, he chooses
for all mankind; a law must be general, it must
not simply apply to a single person. So we must
say that Orestes' law is that it is good to rid
people of their sense of guilt, of their subjec-
tion to moral law. But we can applaud this law
only if we accept the anti–moralistic premisses
of the play; in truth we know that to rid people
of their sense of guilt is to deprive them of
their conscience; and as Orestes capers out at
the end of the play, he leaves behind him a people who are bound to become a prey to their own
self–destructive lawlessness. Therefore the law
on which he acts is not so much a law as a reci-
pe for lawlessness.

If the first mistake made by existentialism
is to slide imperceptibly from the rejection of
everything that is "given", to the rejection of
moral law per se, then its second mistake is its
failure to notice that there are far deadlier

enemies threatening freedom than moralism. Not
the least among them are man's own baser impulses, what Schiller sometimes refers to as his
"crude" nature, the very thing from which moral
law seeks to free man. It was part of the legend
from which Sartre derived the theme of "Les
Mouches" that Orestes belonged to the House of
Atreus, and so, as Electra reminds him, he has
"crime and tragedy" in his blood (Théatre.57).
Possibly this factor has a greater influence on
his behaviour than has his ill-conceived anti-
moralistic philosophy, because as Electra again
points out, as the grandson of Atreus he cannot
escape the "heritage of blood" (Théatre.58).
Taken in a wider sense his heritage is that of
mankind in general, the heritage of the primitive instincts which are a part of human nature,
a heritage which may be leavened and controlled
by moral law, but to which existentialist immoralism opens the floodgates. This may not be
the message which Sartre intended to convey, but
if existentialism is to be foisted into Schiller's idealistic plays, with how much greater
justification may we not inject into Sartre's
existentialist works a little truth and light
to counteract the harm done by his teaching?

We have seen Orestes luxuriating in violence for its own sake, rather than for the sake
of the "freedom" which he associates with it.
The description of freedom which he gives in
appropriately violent terms, when he says that
freedom has "crashed down" on him "like a thun-
derbolt" (Théatre.83), reminds us of the passage
in "Les Chemins de la Liberté" where Daniel, re-
joicing in the collapse of law and order in the
France of 1940, stands in the deserted streets
of Paris startled to see something "hurtling
down from the sky - the ancient law! (C.L.3.82).
But before long the pleasure which Daniel takes
in a deserted Paris where everything is permiss-
ible tends to wear off; sometimes he feels only

a "vast and pointless freedom" (C.L.3.80). We
are also reminded of the occasion when Mathieu
fires down on the Germans from a church tower
(ibid.193). He does so, not in an attempt to
preserve the liberty of his country, but in a
savagely nihilistic mood. Freedom purchased at
the price of law, philanthropy, morality and the
beauty of life, freedom as terror - that is his
freedom. Only after much heart-searching does
Tell commit himself to the use of force: Orestes
and Mathieu exult in violence. It might be arg-
ued that Sartre does not associate himself with
his characters, but neither does he dissociate
himself from them; the violence and the preference for disorder is in "L'Être et le Néant" as
well as in the novels and plays; and since a
critic has appealed to "Les Mouches" as representing Sartre's philosophy in dramatic form, it
is right that we should make quite sure what
that philosophy is, in practice and not merely
in theory, before we compare Sartre's play with
Schiller's.

CHAPTER TWO

DIE JUNGFRAU VON ORLEANS

Anti-idealism such as we have noticed in comments on "Wilhelm Tell" is also a pronounced feature of critiques of "Die Jungfrau von Orleans"; but in this case the bias against idealism manifests itself with a peculiar double effect. Johanna is subjected to adverse criticism so long as she remains faithful to her idealistic mission; but when she begins to falter in that mission, we are told that a new, happier, more harmonious Johanna has come into being.

A typical example of the first type of anti-idealist comment is the criticism of her "failure" to show mercy to Montgomery, and the doubts that are expressed about her "questionable" morality in warfare. The commentators do not lay down any general principles in this matter, but by the peculiar inverted nature of their observations, they raise serious doubts about their own moral philosophy as applied to warfare. Theirs is the topsy-turvy world in which it is right to show pity for the aggressor, and a matter of indifference whether you show pity for the victims of the aggressor. It is a cardinal principle in the morality of warfare that you should go to war only in defence of liberty, and that you should not enter into a war of aggression. A commentator who attaches so little importance to the distinction between aggression and defence that he does not even refer to it, is not exactly qualified to criticise the morality of Johanna, who champions the cause of the victims of aggression. To discuss Johanna's morality in warfare without reference to the fact that she is taking part in a defensive war against an aggressor-nation, or to imagine that

she can win such a war without summoning up all
the relentless determination of which she is capable, is to discuss the matter in terms of complete unreality. Such lack of realism is matched
only by the inconsistency of another type of
commentator who, having referred to the aggressive character of the war waged by the British,
then proceeds to discuss the guilt incurred by
Johanna in opposing the British attempt to sub-
jugate France.

When Montgomery appeals to Johanna in the
name of his parents who are worrying about him
at home, she reminds him of the many French
mothers who, as a result of the war of aggression in which he is participating, have been left
childless; of the many children who have lost
their father, of the many young wives who have
been widowed.

Unglücklicher! Und du erinnerst mich daran,
Wie viele Mütter dieses Landes kinderlos,
Wie viele zarte Kinder vaterlos, wie viel
Verlobte Bräute Witwen worden sind durch
euch! (1628-31)

Her critics turn a blind eye to such passages.
Moved to pity by Montgomery's fear of dying un-
mourned in a foreign land, they have it seems no
pity to spare for the French whose land, as Johanna points out, has been laid waste by the
British army, who have been driven from hearth
and home, and whose towns have been engulfed by
the conflagration of war (1636-9).

Fundamentally the ill-conceived criticism
of Johanna's conduct in the Montgomery episode,
based as it is on the false belief that Schiller
is concerned to bring out a certain character-
defect in Johanna, a regrettable callousness,
is symptomatic of a failure to understand the
two main themes of the play. The first of these
two themes is the mission entrusted to Johanna,
that she shall restore to France the liberty
that is endangered by the British invasion. The

importance of this mission, the fact that it
transcends all other considerations, is brought
out by the references to its spiritual character
("So ist des Geistes Ruf an mich ergangen",399).
Johanna compares this call of the spirit with
the message received by Moses from God through
the burning bush (401ff.). For three nights the
figure of the Virgin Mary appears to her, com-
manding her to abandon her life as a shedherdess
and to take upon herself the task of liberating
France. The wayside shrine where she receives
the message, the sword and the flag borne by the
Virgin Mary, Johanna's own sword obtained from
the place of which she was informed in a vision,
the white flag edged with purple, bearing the
image of the Queen of Heaven with the infant Je-
sus, and the helmet which comes into Johanna's
possession in mysterious circumstances - all
these things, transcending the natural order,
fully attest the divine source of the authority
with which Johanna is invested.

It is an authority by no means discredited
by Thibaut's accusation that she is guilty of
"sinful arrogance" (130), a charge which is immediately refuted by Raimond's reference to her
modesty and her willingness to serve her elder
sisters. The unthinking acceptance of Thibaut's
criticism of Johanna, and the discounting of
Raimond's reply to that criticism, is another
indication of the anti-idealism of a certain
type of commentator. Thibaut's criticism of Johanna is inspired partly by crude peasant superstition (149ff.). We must also take into consideration the peculiar views which he holds concerning the invasion of France: the fortune of
battles is the judgement of God (371), and who-
ever is crowned at Rheims must be accepted as
King (272f.). One wonders whether anyone who adopts such a passive and fatalistic attitude to
the danger that threatens France, has the right
to sit in judgement on his daughter, prepared as

she is to sacrifice both her happiness and her life in rescuing her country.

The divine source of Johanna's authority is intended by Schiller to be accepted as an objective truth, a truth on which the whole action of the play is based. It may be that readers who are not of a religious turn of mind have difficulty in accepting the divine sanction that she enjoys, but they should still be able to accept her idealism, based as it is on the ideal of freedom from foreign domination. As Johanna herself says: "What is innocent, sacred and humanly good, if not the struggle for the fatherland?" (1782f.). If the interpreter cannot or will not accept the idealistic premisses of the play, his interpretation is bound to be ill-founded and misleading.

The other theme, illustrated by the innocent life lived by Johanna at the beginning of the play, might be described as that of pure nature. In Raimond's description she is a modest and pious young woman, quietly obedient in attending to the most burdensome tasks (133-142). E.L.Stahl's description of her as a "beautiful soul" (that is, a person who is by nature virtuous) is not at all invalidated by Thibaut's inability to understand her. It is important to appreciate that this aspect of her character, the pure emotions of sympathy, tenderness and humanity that are natural to her, is not an aspect that is superseded by the theme of her idealistic mission. She continues to be a pure or "beautiful" soul, and from time to time this theme re-emerges at significant moments, particularly in her prayer at the time of her encounter with Montgomery, and even more clearly at the crisis caused by her meeting with Lionel.

There is a conflict in Johanna between her pure nature, that is the pure emotions which are characteristic of her as a simple shepherdess, and on the other hand the idealistic tendency which must have been present in her before she was actually entrusted with the mission of restoring the freedom of France. Love, marriage, children - these are the blessings which, as a pure soul, she would naturally have enjoyed but for the element of idealism in her which causes her to reject the hand of Raimond in marriage.

It is the tension between Johanna's pure emotions and the stern demands of the spirit, between her natural goodness and the means which must be adopted in the interest of the ideal of freedom, which forms the outstanding feature of the play. It is essential that we should bear in mind that nature, pure though it may be in itself, must in Johanna's case be sacrificed to her idealistic mission. It is the failure to understand the need for this sacrifice, that has sometimes led to misinterpretations of the play. Schiller did not write the Montgomery episode as a means of discussing the ethics of warfare or Johanna's "questionable" conduct in battle. He wrote it as one of a series of four tests or trials which she has to undergo, to illustrate the necessity of subordinating her pure emotions to the exigencies of the military campaign. The danger to which Johanna is exposed in the war is not that she might display hard-heartedness to the enemy, but on the contrary that owing to her pure nature, the natural sympathy and humanity with which she is endowed, she might prove to be too soft-hearted for the rigours of warfare. Schiller has in fact two purposes: to show in the first place that she is still capable of being moved by pure emotions, and in the second place that these emotions must not become a disadvantage to her in her military pursuits.

Johanna's opponent is sometimes described as the "helpless" Montgomery, but in what sense is he at a disadvantage vis-à-vis Johanna? He is a trained and experienced soldier. He throws away his sword, but Johanna generously gives him

an opportunity to retrieve it. Before they en-
gage in combat, Montgomery so far recovers his
courage as to express the hope that he may, as
he puts it (1672), "send her to hell". Nor is
the result of the combat by any means a foregone
conclusion; just before it commences, Johanna in
one of her prophetic moments declares that she
will never return to her beloved homeland, but
will herself perish in battle (1666f.), a proph-
ecy which later in the play proves to be true.
In no sense is Montgomery a special case; if Johanna were to spare his life, she might just as
well spare the life of every soldier in the
British army.

If Johanna had indeed spared Montgomery's
life, would he have withdrawn from the war and
returned to his native land? He would not have
dared to do so; for he has witnessed Talbot's
action in striking down a man caught in the act
of fleeing, and he would not have wished to experience a similar fate. It is therefore likely
that Montgomery would have continued to act as
a combattant in the battle.

The "helpless" Montgomery shows an uncanny
understanding of where Johanna's weakness, from
a military point of view, is to be found; for he
sets out to "soften" her heart by an appeal to
her emotions.

Ob ich vielleicht durch Tränen sie erweichen
                      kann! (1579)

Although Johanna does her best, as Shakespeare
has it, to "disguise fair nature with hard-fav-
our'd rage", she does not altogether succeed in
concealing her emotions; and Montgomery does not
fail to notice that, fierce though her speech
may be, her glance is gentle (1603). So he persists, appealing first to the tenderness and
sensitivity that is characteristic of her sex,
and then to her understanding of the bond of
love that makes him long to return home. When
she replies that beneath her armour there beats

no heart ("Dieser Panzer deckt kein Herz",1611), she is describing the condition which she seeks to induce in herself during the battle, rather than a condition that is characteristic of her. She refers nostalgically to her earlier life of pure nature, when instead of a sword, she carried the "pious" shepherd's crook (1657), and her tender emotions are clearly revealed when she speaks of the sacrifice which she has had to make in tearing herself away from her dear sisters (1659). It affords her no pleasure to take up the sword and to strike down the aggressor (1658ff.). Further evidence of Johanna's "fair nature" is to be found in her prayer to the Virgin Mary in 2.8.

In Mitleid schmilzt die Seele und die Hand
                              erbebt,
Als bräche sie in eines Tempels heilgen Bau,
Den blühenden Leib des Gegners zu verletzen,
Schon vor des Eisens blanker Schneide
                    schaudert mir... (1680ff.)

"My soul melts with pity and my hand trembles, as though it were breaking into the sacred precinct of a temple, to wound the fair body of my adversary; seeing the bright edge of the blade, I shudder." These are the words, not of an unfeeling or merciless person, but of a woman who has the understanding and good sense to see that when you are fighting for the freedom of your country against the aggressor, you cannot always afford to show mercy. Presumably Schiller was relying on his interpreters to have the same understanding and good sense. If the "strength" and the "implacability" which Johanna refers to as coming to her from above, is disturbing –

Erhabne Jungfrau, du wirkst Mächtiges
                              in mir!
Du rüstest den unkriegerischen Arm mit Kraft,
Dies Herz mit Unerbittlichkeit bewaffnest du.
                    (1677-9)

– perhaps the triumph which the aggressor would

have celebrated if these qualities had not been
forthcoming, would have been considered by the
commentator to be still more disturbing.

Just as in her first trial Johanna overcomes the danger that she might succumb to the
pity which she feels for the aggressor, so in
her second trial in 3.4. she rejects the suggestion that she should allow herself to be di-
verted from her task of prosecuting the war, by
contracting a marriage with Dunois or La Hire.
If she were to marry she would be disobeying the
divine injunction mentioned in her monologue in
the Prologue.

Nicht Männerliebe darf dein Herz berühren.
                                        (411)
But quite apart from that injunction, it would
be an act of great folly to interrupt her life-
-and-death struggle with the invaders, in order
to marry one of her two suitors, to neither of
whom she is drawn by any feeling of affection.

Each of the three trials Johanna successfully undergoes contains a rebuke which she solemnly administers to the person who is seeking
to divert her from her idealistic mission. In
the scene with Montgomery it is her speech beginning "Wer rief euch in das fremde Land...?"
(1636). In the second trial, in which she is
tempted with the idea of marriage, her rebuke is
contained in the speech beginning: "Dauphin!
Bist du der göttlichen Erscheinung schon müde?"
(2247). "Are you so weary of the divine revela-
tion that you would destroy its vessel, dragging
down to the common dust the pure maiden whom God
has sent to you? You blind hearts! O you of little faith! Heaven's glory shines about you, re-
vealing its wonders to you, and you see nothing
but a woman in me." Johanna speaks with authority, her words express so to speak the spiritual
message of the play, and the rebuke she administers is well deserved. In this passage Schiller
clearly expresses his sense of the disproportion

between the idealist's vision and the materialistic thoughts of those who can but imperfectly
comprehend that vision.

As regards the third trial, common sense is
needed in judging Schiller's intention in introducing the sinister figure of the Black Knight.
It would not have made sense if he had employed
the Black Knight to warn Johanna against the
danger of hubris in going too far in prosecuting
her campaign against the English invaders; for
if she had stopped half way in fulfilling her
mission, this would have demonstrated, not her
moderation, but simply her failure to bring her
mission to a successful conclusion. What happens
when, as a result of her encounter with Lionel,
she is indeed prevented from continuing the campaign, shows that the advice given by the Black
Knight cannot be the wise and objective counsel
of a friendly spirit, but is on the contrary the
ill-intentioned prompting of a hostile spirit;
for as the charcoal-burner's wife complains, the
invaders quickly recover the initiative and re-
impose their oppressive rule on the French peasants (3066ff.). Additional support for the interpretation of the Black Knight as a hostile
spirit is given by Schiller's statement that he
would have no objection if the Knight were iden-
tified with the recently departed Talbot (NA.
Vol.9.433). In this third trial an attempt is
made to undermine Johanna's wholehearted dedication to her idealistic mission by playing upon
the materialistic hopes and fears that are common to human beings; but Johanna for her part,
successfully resisting the temptation, declares
her determination to complete her work and re-
deem her vow, rebuking the Black Knight in the
following passage.

Was heißest du in Mitte meines Laufs
Mich stille stehen und mein Werk verlassen?
Ich führ es aus und löse mein Gelübde!
(2426-8)

Thus Johanna's rejection of the materialistic considerations advanced by the Black Knight represents a triumph for her dedication to her idealistic mission. She has already gained a similar triumph in repudiating the ridiculous suggestion that she should hold up the military campaign in order to contract a loveless and therefore a pointless marriage. As for her encounter with Montgomery, those who cannot understand the statement that her idealism has triumphed in that episode too, should consider for a moment what would have become of her idealistic mission, if she had allowed her pity for the aggressor to weaken her determination to frustrate his aggressive purposes.

It is in her fourth trial that the play reaches its climax; for here, in Act 3, Scene 10 she falls in love with Lionel, one of the British commanders, and although she has him at her mercy, she allows him to live to fight another day. There surely cannot be many critics who fail to understand that her sense of guilt and bewilderment, expressed in the following lines, arises from her awareness that, in failing to overcome her love of Lionel and in sparing his life, she betrays her mission.

Und bin ich strafbar, weil ich menschlich
                              war?
Ist Mitleid Sünde?-Mitleid! Hörtest du
Des Mitleids Stimme und der Menschlichkeit
Auch bei den andern, die dein Schwert
                              geopfert?
Warum verstummte sie, als der Walliser dich,
Der zarte Jüngling, um sein Leben flehte?
Arglistig Herz! Du lügst dem ewgen Licht,
Dich trieb des Mitleids fromme Stimme nicht!
                  (2567-74)

At first she is inclined to associate the attraction that she feels for Lionel with the pure or "pious" feeling of pity, and this leads her to sound a note of protest against the need

to suppress the emotions of pure nature. Is it
reprehensible, she asks, to show humanity and
pity? The answer given in the play is that such
emotions, although in themselves they represent
pure nature, are to be suppressed whenever they
conflict with her mission. Her reference to pity
serves to link the Lionel episode, where love
plays its part, with the Montgomery scene, and
to bring out the fact that in both scenes Johanna has the same difficulty to overcome, that
of controlling "pure nature", whether it takes
the form of pity or love.

When Johanna states that she did not in
fact hear the voice of pity and humanity in her
combat with Montgomery, what she implies is that
she was not prevented by those emotions from
fulfilling her military duty and remaining true
to her mission; her prayer to the Virgin Mary is
proof that she did in fact feel pity for Montgomery, but that she succeeded in suppressing it
as incompatible with her mission. Dismayed at
her failure to suppress her feeling of love for
Lionel, as she suppressed the pity that she felt
for Montgomery, Johanna owing to her sense of
guilt comes to suspect that the former emotion
is somehow less "pious" or pure than that of
pity. Therefore she accuses herself of betraying
the "eternal light" (2573).

But there is more than one way in which Johanna is exposed to this danger, since she may
betray the light not only through experiencing
feelings which are less pure than the "pious
voice of pity", but also in the way which she
experienced with Montgomery, through feelings of
pity and humanity which, however pure in themselves, may weaken her whole-hearted dedication
to her mission. Therefore, having expressed her
doubts about her feelings for Lionel, Johanna
returns to the main theme of the play, the in-
compatibility of feelings of pure nature with
the mission entrusted to her.

Would the play have been made more inter-
esting if, in accordance with the views of certain critics, Schiller had portrayed a "new" Johanna as coming to life through her love of
Lionel: a Johanna who is no longer "obstinately
committed" to her idealistic mission, who has
more sympathy with ordinary people, a sympathy
which extends even to the British, whom she recognises as having their own valid point of view?
In short would it have been better if Schiller
had represented Johanna's love of Lionel, with
which she betrays her mission, as a blessing in
disguise? It is one thing for a commentator to
speculate along these lines; it is a very different thing for him to pretend that this is more
or less what Schiller has written. It is the
difference between the germ of an idea for a new
play on the same subject, and on the other hand
a misinterpretation of the play that Schiller
actually wrote.

In fact however Johanna is portrayed in Act
Four as very different from the "happy" Johanna
described by the type of commentator referred
to. For a short time, when she is temporarily
reunited with her sisters, Louison and Margot,
she is able to recapture the happiness she knew
as a shepherdess in her home village (2898ff.).
But she is able to do so only by misrepresenting
the guilt that she has incurred as arising, not
from her failure to suppress her feelings for
Lionel, but from the mission itself, which she
momentarily repudiates as an act of hubris for
which she must atone (2933-8).

Apart from the fond illusion she cherishes
awhile during her reunion with her sisters, the
illusion that she might return to her past life,
her main feelings are those of bitter remorse
and utter despair at her inability to "harden
her heart" in her encounter with Lionel,i.e. to
suppress the pure emotion of love which, as she
says, heaven itself created, but which she (on

account of the mission which it is her duty to
fulfil) is obliged to forgo.

Konnt ich dieses Herz verhärten,
Das der Himmel fühlend schuf! (2596f.)

This is the moment in the play which brings out
most clearly the tension between her feelings as
a "beautiful soul" and the mission that has been
entrusted to her by God. It is also a moment
which underlines the mistake made by those commentators who criticise Johanna, not for failing
to harden her heart in the scene with Lionel,
but for her refusal to soften it in the scene
with Montgomery. Johanna is so far from believing that emotions of love and pity are compati-
ble with the martial virtues, that she makes a
moving appeal to God to employ his own celestial
spirits, immune to feeling, as instruments of
His divine will, rather than the "gentle soul of
the shepherdess".

Deine Geister sende aus,
Die Unsterblichen, die Reinen,
Die nicht fühlen, die nicht weinen!
Nicht die zarte Jungfrau wähle,
Nicht der Hirtin weiche Seele! (2601-5)

Irony of the cruellest kind is employed in
4.2., the scene between Johanna and Agnes Sorel,
who ignorant of what has happened between Johanna and Lionel, urges her to feel the pure emotion of love. Agnes is unaware that her words
can only have the effect of increasing Johanna's
distress; for the joy of pure love, which she
commends to her, is an emotion to which Johanna
(having regard to the requirements of her mission) is all too ready to respond. Indeed Johanna
bitterly reproaches herself for having already
betrayed her mission by yielding to that emotion
(2712f.). So far removed is she from the commentators' false image of a "new" and "happy" Johanna, that when she is told, after being captured, that she is to be taken to Lionel, she
begs rather to be put to death (3225f.). We are

sometimes told that there is a more accommodating note in the words which she addresses to him in 5.9., but those who maintain that this is so, usually prefer not to support their contention with a quotation.

> Du bist
> Der Feind mir, der verhaßte, meines Volks.
> Nichts kann gemein sein zwischen dir und mir.
> Nicht lieben kann ich dich, doch wenn dein
> Herz
> Sich zu mir neigt, so laß es Segen bringen
> Für unsre Völker.-Führe deine Heere
> Hinweg von meines Vaterlandes Boden...
> (3348-54)

He is her "hateful enemy", there can be nothing in common between them, and she cannot love him. The reference to the possibility that his affection for Johanna might prove to be a blessing to their two nations, leads only to her insistence that he must withdraw his armies from the soil of France. Thus the only concession which she makes is an appeal that Lionel should withdraw his forces voluntarily; but if he will not do so, he will be forced to withdraw them.

> Tu es bei Zeiten, denn du mußt es doch.(3361)

We see that Johanna's "obsession" with her mission is by no means a thing of the past; nor is her faith in the inspiration that comes to her from God. The critic who discovers her in a temporary mood of despondency which overcomes her when she is told that she is to be sent to Lionel, and who quotes her words at this moment as though they were typical of her attitude -

> Kein Gott erscheint, kein Engel zeigt sich
> mehr,
> Die Wunder ruhn, der Himmel ist verschlossen.
> (3244f.)

- does a disservice to the truth. When Thibaut makes his dramatic challenge -

> Gehörst du zu den Heiligen und Reinen? (2985)

- she could easily have denied the imputation

that she is in league with the devil, but she
prefers to expose herself to public disgrace,
accepting this as a penance for having temporarily failed in her mission. She later tells Raimond that her public disgrace was providential
("eine Schickung", 3156), and that she has si-
lently submitted to the fate which God has imposed on her (3147).

In Act 5 she is as conscious of being guided by God as she is in Act 1. Even in her period
in the wilderness after she has been rejected by
the court as a witch, she speaks to Raimond of
her sense of being accompanied by God. Fate is
guiding her, and she is confident that she will
accomplish her mission almost without any effort
on her part (because she is God's instrument).

Ich bin nicht unbegleitet.
Du hast den Donner über mir gehört.
Mein Schicksal führt mich. Sorge nicht,
                    ich werde
Ans Ziel gelangen, ohne daß ichs suche.(3113)
When Raimond expresses his astonishment that Johanna, though innocent, should suffer banishment
uncomplainingly, she replies that she would not
deserve to be God's missionary, if she did not
unhesitatingly accept His will.

Verdient ichs, die Gesendete zu sein,
Wenn ich nicht blind des Meisters Willen
                    ehrte! (3165f.)
Finally let us complete the evidence of her continuing faith in God with the words with which
she assures Raimond that she has seen the Eternal with her own eyes.

Ich habe das Unsterbliche mit Augen
Gesehen... (3191f.)
So the evidence of the text demonstrates beyond
any doubt that Johanna has by no means lost her
faith in God. When she speaks of having been
"cured" ("Jetzt bin ich/ Geheilt", 3174f.), her
words have been misconstrued as meaning that she
has been cured of her "sanctity", which is said

to have been replaced by "sanity". Yet Johanna's
reference to her "cure" occurs in 5.4., from
which we have extracted our last three passages
quoted to demonstrate her continuing religious
faith. It would be preposterous to suppose that
Johanna, who has throughout the play drawn her
inspiration from God, would now speak of having
been cured of her faith. On the contrary the
loss of such inspiration would have reduced her
to utter despair. The context makes it clear
that it is a certain weakness within herself, of
which she has been cured: her love of Lionel
which has impeded her in fulfilling her mission.

Ich bin mir keiner Schwachheit mehr bewußt!
(3179)

There is no avoiding the main theme of the play,
the conflict between Johanna's heart and her
mind, between her tender feelings and the stern
call of the spirit. If a commentator is entirely
preoccupied with the ideal of the "beautiful
soul", in whom heart and mind, sense and spirit
are in harmony, he will necessarily be out of
touch with the leading theme of the work; for
whereas Johanna is called upon to achieve sublimity by subordinating her emotional life to
the demands of the spirit, the commentator who
is obsessed with a theory of wholeness and harmony will for ever be attempting to fasten this
theory, however attractive it may be in itself,
on a play where it is quite out of place. Evidence of course is required, and evidence of a
kind is forthcoming. As Johanna lies dying in
5.14., she is compared by Burgund to an "angel"
or a "sleeping child".

Seht einen Engel scheiden! Seht, wie sie da
liegt,
Schmerzlos und ruhig wie ein schlafend Kind!
(3508f.)

Such is the flimsy evidence on which the critic
must rely in attempting to prove his mistaken
thesis. But we have seen the conflict between

Johanna's pure emotions and her commitment to her spiritual mission; we have seen her achieve sublimity in subordinating her emotions to her idealistic goal; and we would require more substantial evidence than the conventional tribute of an epitaph if we were to believe that it is not sublimity, but harmony that is the ruling principle of the play.

We must judge the state of Johanna's heart and mind by the evidence of the play itself, not by a passage in Schiller's "Letters on the Aesthetic Education of Man" in which he says that "man must learn to desire more nobly, in order that he may not need to will sublimely" (Letter XXIII.8.NA.Vol.20.388). Johanna is in no need of instruction in the art of desiring nobly; for she is already a noble or pure soul. Furthermore the situation in which she finds herself positively calls for sublimity of will. Another passage in the same Letter is far more relevant to Johanna. "Only the challenge of a sublime situation", says Schiller, "is needed to transform aesthetic man" (or by implication the pure soul) "into the hero and the sage" (NA.385). The mistake made by the commentator who would have Johanna address herself above all to the cultivation of her beautiful soul, is that he ignores the situation in which she finds herself in the play. It is, to use Schiller's phrase, a "sublime situation", that is a situation which calls for sublimity, since nothing less can enable Johanna to defeat the aggressor and restore France to her liberty.

In an ideal world where aggression would be ruled out because everyone would live in accordance with his pure nature, there would be no need of a St.Joan to display sublimity in rescuing her country. In the meantime, until all nations have learned to "desire more nobly", to cultivate their pure nature, there will always be a need for a "sublime" deliverer to oppose

the ignoble desires of men. This does not seem
to be understood by the type of commentator to
whom we have been referring.

So while Johanna is sublimely concerned to
save the people of France, giving not a thought
to herself, the commentator, seemingly indifferent to the fate of France, is quite unnecessar-
ily concerned about the condition of Johanna's
soul, which can be relied upon to take care of
itself, so long as Johanna remains dedicated to
her mission. Such commentators tend to discount
the harsh realities of the play, the brute fact
that the British are waging a war of aggression
against France. They live in a world of make-
believe in which normal human relations exist
between the aggressors and their victims; in
which Johanna can afford to yield to the pity
which she feels for Montgomery, and to indulge
her affection for Lionel. Indeed such critics
have not a little in common with King Charles
himself, who at the beginning of the play, at a
time when France is in danger of collapsing before the British onslaught, would like nothing
better than to emulate the King of Naples in
dreaming of constructing an "innocently pure
world in this crude barbaric reality" (511-5).

There has been a certain tendency among
anti-idealist writers to set up Talbot as a ri-
val to Johanna. He appears in only five scenes,
three of which are insignificant. His claim that
the English campaign in France is justified, is
a mere assertion without any attempt to substan-
tiate it (1395f.). Not only is Talbot an alien
conqueror; he also exploits the unnatural divis-
ions that have arisen among the French. Of the
two scenes that are slightly more significant,
Act 2, Scene 5 serves only to show how completely at a loss Talbot is to understand the moral
and spiritual strength of Johanna (1538-48). The
type of commentator who makes such a point of
criticising Johanna's "questionable" conduct in

warfare, manages to turn a blind eye to Talbot's
action, at the end of this scene, in striking
down one of his own men.
  In the last scene in which Talbot appears,
Act 3, Scene 6, he is mortally wounded. Rheims
has been lost. The war continues to go against
him. He awaits his death in complete disillu-
sionment.In this mood he delivers himself of the
following lines.
  Unsinn, du siegst und ich muß untergehn!
  Mit der Dummheit kämpfen Götter selbst
                              vergebens.
  Erhabene Vernunft...
  Wer bist du denn, wenn du dem tollen Roß
  Des Aberwitzes an den Schweif gebunden,
  Ohnmächtig rufend, mit dem Trunkenen
  Dich sehend in den Abgrund stürzen mußt!
  Verflucht sei, wer sein Leben an das Große
  Und Würdge wendet und bedachte Pläne
  Mit weisem Geist entwirft! (2318-29)
It would perhaps be somewhat naive of us, if
after reading Talbot's reference to his having
devoted his life to whatever is "great and worthy" (2327f.), we were to complain that there is
no evidence in the play of his having done anything of the kind. As we can see from the vocab-
ulary which he and Lionel employ, theirs is the
"greatness" of the professional soldier. Fame to
them is the "glory of victory" ("Siegesruhm",
1548), a "hero" (1547) is a person who wins battles, and to lose a battle is to suffer "disgrace" ("Schimpf", 1464). Talbot's view of warfare is entirely amoral, as is shown by the concept of "honour" (1240) which he and Lionel
share: it is a concept which has nothing to do
with ethics, and everything to do with the winning of battles. While commentators presume to
question Johanna's morality in warfare, it never
occurs to Talbot that there is such a thing, except in the sense that it is one's moral duty
to win: he knows no distinction between defence

and aggression. He has no conception of fighting not just as a way of life, but for a cause; to fight as Johanna fights, for a noble ideal, for freedom, for France, for God, is to fight for a goal which quite transcends the greed for territorial aggrandisement, the military "glory" which is his be-all and end-all.

Since the morality of the war is all on Johanna's side (because she is fighting in defence against aggression), how does it come about that Talbot arrogates to himself an idealistic rôle, claiming (by implication) that he has acted as the champion of "sublime reason" (2320)? Condemning and despising his own soldiers for attributing to Johanna the supernatural qualities of a witch, he is not above making use of her reputation as a witch in order to discredit her. He seeks to tarnish her reputation by associating it with all that is irrational - with "nonsense" ("Unsinn"), "stupidity" ("Dummheit"), "superstition" ("Aberwitz") and "jugglery" ("Gaukelkunst"). He himself, by way of contrast, is to be associated with all that is rational, with "sublime reason". In appealing to this quality he is making a vain gesture: despite the immoralism of his war-making, he claims a virtue which he does not possess, in order that he may not die unconsoled. He is superior to the force that has destroyed him: that belief is his consolation.

Now let us look at the claims that are made on Talbot's behalf by those whose purpose is to discredit Johanna. Partly on the strength of his death-bed conversion to the idea of "sublime reason", he is made the focal point of certain "rational" values opposed to what is called the "irrationalism" of Johanna. Apart from that late reference to "sublime reason", what else is there in the play which might be appealed to in an attempt to justify the belief that Talbot represents reason in opposition to Johanna's

"unreason"? The argument seems to go like this.
(1) The British soldiers flee from Johanna as
from a witch.
(2) Therefore Johanna is guilty of taking
advantage of irrational superstition.
(3) Talbot reacts furiously against the
superstitious awe in which his men hold Johanna.
(4) Therefore he is the champion of "rational-
ism" as against Johanna's "irrationalism".

It is of such non sequiturs that legends
are created; and lo and behold, before we know
it, we have a "dialectic" in the play, and in
this dialectic Talbot is said to enjoy a certain
"integrity" (whatever that is intended to mean
in reference to such an aggressor) equal to that
of Johanna; he is even said to reveal the "ambiguity" of the idealist, to draw attention to a
certain shadow side of Johanna's character.

If ever there was an unambiguous idealist,
it is Johanna; her shadow side exists only in
the muddled thoughts of commentators who have
grossly misinterpreted the Montgomery episode,
and have distorted the significance of Talbot.
The only "shadow" that falls over the play is
cast by the war of aggression waged by Talbot,
and opposed by Johanna with her own radiant idealism. It is not from any "shadow side" in Johanna's character, that the crisis of the play
arises in the scene with Lionel, but from her
tender loving side, that "fair nature" which in
itself, dissociated from the conditions of her
idealistic mission, is represented as pure, as
good. To elevate Talbot, who as the aggressor
himself embodies the shadow side of human nature, to a position of equality with Johanna,
who sacrifices herself in opposing that shadow
side, is a remarkable misinterpretation of the
play.

As he lies dying in Act 3, Scene 6, contemplating the thought of his disintegrating body
and the handful of dust that will soon be all

that is left of him, Talbot presents a picture
of utter spiritual bankruptcy.

> ...von dem mächtigen Talbot, der die Welt
> Mit seinem Kriegsruhm füllte, bleibt nichts
> übrig,
> Als eine Handvoll leichten Staubs. (2349-51)

Even if it were true that his life had been devoted to whatever is "sublime and desirable",
his final insight is the vanity of all such aspiration.

> ...die Einsicht in das Nichts,
> Und herzliche Verachtung alles dessen,
> Was uns erhaben schien und wünschenswert.
> (2354-6)

Thus in the manner of his dying Talbot provides
an appropriately inglorious foil to the splended
apotheosis of Johanna in the closing moments of
the play.

CHAPTER THREE

DON KARLOS

It is an obvious and well-known paradox of Schiller's "Don Karlos" that Marquis Posa, the idealistic opponent of the despotism presided over by King Philipp of Spain, himself develops despotic tendencies. Surprised as he is to discover in his audience with the King in Act 3, Scene 10, that the latter is not altogether unresponsive to his appeal to humanity, Posa even comes to believe in the possibility of realising his political ideals and of bringing about the liberation of Flanders from Spanish rule, by actually converting the despotic monarch to his own faith in freedom. "Now it is with him as with every fanatic who is overwhelmed by his ruling idea", Schiller writes in his sixth Letter on "Don Karlos"; "he no longer knows any limits".

Jetzt ergeht es ihm wie jedem Schwärmer, der von seiner herrschenden Idee überwältigt wird. Er kennt keine Grenzen mehr...
(NA.22.156)

There follows the bizarre sequence of actions which form the main outward events of the last two Acts: Posa becomes the King's Minister without explaining his purpose either to Don Karlos or to the Queen, he shows the King the Prince's correspondence, he arranges for Don Karlos to be arrested, and he all but stabs Princess Eboli to death. These things he does with the most impeccable motives, but in an atmosphere of secrecy which leaves his friends utterly bewildered.

The theme of the "sacrifice" is first introduced in reference to the inhumanity of the despotism of King Philipp. The burning of heretics greatly disturbs the Queen in Act 1, Scene 3, but

her attendants regard the auto-da-fé as a pro-
per part of Christianity. However, after Princess Eboli has defended the practice, a reference to the prospect of an arranged marriage for
her, causes her to appeal to the Queen to prevent her from being "sacrificed".
Um Gottes willen, lassen Sie mich nicht -
Nicht aufgeopfert werden. (450f.)
(The quotations are from the 1805 version, un-
less otherwise stated.)
    The Queen knows that it is a "hard fate" to
be thus sacrificed; for she herself was engaged
to be married to Don Karlos before she was required to marry the King. The theme is continued
in the next scene, where Posa tells the tragic
story of Mathilde who, though engaged to Fernan-
do, was obliged to marry the powerful Pietro.
Under the despotic system presided over by King
Philipp II and the Grand Inquisitor, the emotions of the human heart are as unimportant as
freedom of conscience. When the Inquisitor ob-
jects to the King's action in having Posa shot,
his complaint relates, not to the act of "sacrifice" in itself, but to the fact that Posa ought
to have been handed over to the Church to be
dealt with.
    Was vermochte Sie, dies Opfer   ·
Dem heil'gen Amt zu unterschlagen? (5167)
    But the image of the "sacrifice" is also
employed to suggest a parallel between Posa's
despotic tendency and the prevailing despotism
of King Philipp; for the intrigues entered into
by Posa cause Don Karlos and the Queen to feel
that they are being "sacrificed" by the very
person on whose sense of humanity they believed
they could rely. When Don Karlos hears from Ler-
ma's lips of Posa's dealings with the King, he
is convinced that he is being sacrificed to the
millions of people to whom Posa hopes to give
liberty.
Doch sollen Millionen ihm, soll ihm

Das Vaterland nicht teurer sein als einer?
                                    (3969)
Attempting to look at the matter dispassionate-
ly, Don Karlos almost succeeds in persuading
himself that since Posa's heart is too big for
mere friendship, he is perhaps right to sacrifice his friend to his "virtue" (an expression
which is sometimes used to denote idealism).
  Sein Busen war für einen Freund zu groß...
  Er opferte mich seiner Tugend.(3971-3)
But when Don Karlos has been thrown into prison
by Posa, a new note of irony is heard as he says
that Posa's idealism (again suggested by "Tugend") could never be cruel or inhuman: Posa's
tender heart must have bled for his sacrifice,
as he adorned him for the altar.
  Hart kann die Tugend sein, doch grausam nie,
  Unmenschlich nie - Es hat dir viel gekostet!
  O ja, mir deucht, ich weiß recht gut,wie sehr
  Geblutet hat dein sanftes Herz, als du
  Dein Opfer schmücktest zum Altare.(4501-5)
The Queen complains that Posa, using the love
with which she inspires Don Karlos as a means of
stimulating his idealism, tends to forget that
she for her part possesses a woman's heart,which
deserves some consideration.
                    Glaubten Sir
  Im Ernst mich aller Weiblichkeit entbunden,
  Da Sie zu seinem Engel mich gemacht,
  Zu seinen Waffen Tugend ihm gegeben?(4344-7)
Don Karlos, concerned for the Queen, asks Posa
whether it was necessary that she should also be
sacrificed. Again the note of irony creeps in
as he remarks that Posa, with his strict idealism, could scarcely be expected to share his
trifling concern for his beloved.
                    Mußte sie
  Das zweite Opfer sein?....
  ....Soll deine strenge Tugend
  Die kleinen Sorgen meiner Liebe fragen?(4531)
    Posa's failure to act in the spirit of his

own ideal of freedom has provided the anti-
idealistic and pro-existentialist school of lit-
erary interpretation with an excuse to speak of
Schiller's "negative judgement" of the type of
the idealist, to maintain that "idealism is rejected" in this play (K.H.40). After quoting
from Schiller's critique of Posa at the end of
the Eleventh "Letter" on "Don Karlos", in which
the playwright speaks of the danger, in moral
matters, of departing from "natural practical
feeling" and of entrusting oneself to the "guidance of universal ideas of reason", the critic
goes on to associate Schiller's comment with the
principle of modern existentialism that "existence precedes essence" (ibid,41). Let us therefore examine what Schiller says in the Eleventh
"Letter", in order that we may consider whether
his reference to the importance of "natural
practical feeling" and other such references
amount to a commendation of existentialism in
preference to idealism.

Diese meine ich, daß man sich in moralischen
Dingen nicht ohne Gefahr von dem natürlichen
praktischen Gefühl entfernt, um sich zu allgemeinen Abstraktionen zu erheben, daß sich
der Mensch weit sicherer den Eingebungen
seines Herzens oder dem schon gegenwärtigen
und individuellen Gefühle von Recht und Unrecht vertraut als der gefährlichen Leitung
universeller Vernunftideen, die er sich
künstlich erschaffen hat – denn nichts führt
zum Guten, was nicht natürlich ist.

(NA.22.172)

"I am of the opinion that it is not without danger that one departs, in moral matters, from
natural practical feeling, in order to rise to
the level of general abstractions; that it is
far safer for man to rely on the inspiration of
his heart, or on the already present and individual sense of right and wrong, than on the
dangerous guidance of universal ideas of reason,

which he has artificially created for himself –
for nothing that is not natural leads to what is
good."

In quoting this passage, the critic stops
short before reaching Schiller's concluding reference to the importance of what is "natural".
The passage as a whole, with its appeal to "natural practical feeling", the "inspiration of the
heart", the "already present and individual
sense of right and wrong", and lastly the statement that only what is natural leads to what is
good, makes it clear that what Schiller is com-
mending is nothing remotely resembling existentialism, but on the contrary a philosophy of
nature. In view of the immoralism of existentialism, there could scarcely be a philosophy
more opposed to existentialism than Schiller's
philosophy of nature; for in appealing to the
principle of nature, Schiller invokes the morally "pure" nature to which he refers for instance
in his study of naive and sentimental poetry
(NA.20.436). A true human being, says Schiller
in "Über Anmut und Würde", should be able to
rely on his own natural impulses for moral guidance, without having to refer to a moral principle. A "beautiful soul" is thus a person in whom
"the moral sense has taken control of all human
emotions to such a degree that it can safely en-
trust the control of the will to the emotion".

"Eine schöne Seele nennt man es, wenn sich
das sittliche Gefühl aller Empfindungen des Menschen endlich bis zu dem Grad versichert hat,
daß es dem Affekt die Leitung des Willens ohne
Scheu überlassen darf. (NA.20.287)

In "Don Karlos" there are two characters
who are deserving of the title of "beautiful
soul". Of Don Karlos himself Schiller writes as
follows in the 9th of the Letters on the play.

"At a corrupt moral court he has retained
the purity of original innocence; neither his
love nor any endeavour by means of principles,

but simply and solely his moral instinct has
preserved him from impurity."

"An einem verderbten, sittenlosen Hofe hat
er die Reinigkeit der ersten Unschuld erhalten;
nicht seine Liebe, auch nicht Anstrengung durch
Grundsätze, ganz allein moralischer Instinkt hat
ihn vor dieser Befleckung bewahrt." (NA.22.165)
"Moral instinct", a phrase also employed in the
first of the "Letters on the Aesthetic Education
of Man", is a variant of "pure nature", implying
as it does that nature has its own moral principle. The most conspicuous example of a "schöne
Seele" in the play is the Queen.The type of virtue exemplified by Princess Eboli's conduct is
used simply to set off the Queen's very different kind of virtue; for in the case of Princess
Eboli virtue is a matter of "education, principle, name it as you will; it is an acquired innocence, extracted from her hot blood by cunning
and arduous exercises".

Erziehung, Grundsatz, nenn' es wie du willst,
Erworbne Unschuld, dem erhitzten Blut
Durch List und schwere Kämpfe abgerungen...
                (2339-41)
"Education", "moral principle", "acquired innocence" - these are expressions which refer to a
form of virtue which does not arise from nature
and could not truly be described as "pure nature" or "moral instinct". The Queen's virtue on
the other hand is described as "innate".

In angeborner stiller Glorie,
Mit sorgenlosem Leichtsinn, mit des Anstands
Schulmäßiger Berechnung unbekannt,
Gleich ferne von Verwegenheit und Furcht,
Mit festem Heldenschritte wandelt sie
Die schmale Mittelbahn des Schicklichen...
                (2356-61)
The Queen, equally free from impropriety (sug-
gested by "Leichtsinn" and "Verwegenheit"") and
from moral coercion ("des Anstands schulmäßige
Berechnung"), treads the "narrow central path of

propriety", because her morality is rooted in
pure nature.
     In Schiller's philosophy the idea of nature
is not opposed to the rational-moral principle,
but allied with it. If therefore, in the Letters
on the play, Schiller invokes the principle of
nature in order to counteract a certain false
tendency, this false tendency cannot be idealism
itself, because in Schiller's philosophy nature
(that is, pure nature) is neither anti-rational-
alistic nor anti-idealistic; it must be an aberration of idealism to which he refers, in fact
precisely the "Schwärmerei" or fanaticism which
he criticises in Posa.
     Once Posa has decided to work through the
King and fails to keep Don Karlos and the Queen
in his confidence, ignoring their natural feelings, he is in fact guilty of adopting a method
which is not natural and therefore not good.
Posa himself openly admits his fault when he
confesses to Don Karlos that he "forgot his
heart", and that it is for this reason that his
idealistic plans have collapsed about him.
          Mein Gebäude stürzt
     Zusammen - ich vergaß dein Herz. (4526)
But Schiller's criticism of Posa properly refers
to the methods he employs, not to his aims. Posa
believes in the ideals of political freedom,
freedom of thought and religion, freedom of conscience. Are these ideals to be rejected simply
because he goes astray in the methods he employs
to realise them? Posa expresses the noble idealism of youth, he utters that idealistic yearning
for liberty, that love of mankind, which is the
characteristic note of the play and is found in
the same measure in no other play written by
Schiller. All this is acknowledged by Schiller
in the Eleventh Letter, where he says that he
"chose an entirely well-meaning character, free
from any selfish desire", that he "gave him the
greatest respect for the rights of others" and

"represented his purpose as that of bringing
about a general enjoyment of liberty"(NA.Vol.22.
172). We should bear this in mind in judging the
critic's assertion that Schiller in this play
"rejects idealism".
In general, apart from the change which
occurs in his policy as a result of his audience
with the King, it is precisely upon nature that
Posa's idealistic plans are based. Just as in
Schiller's philosophical writings nature, far
from being opposed to idealism, is its natural
ally, so in this play we see the pure nature of
love and friendship dedicated to the service of
idealism; it is upon such pure nature and its
capacity to ascend to the level of idealism that
Posa relies. Man's pure nature, those unselfish
emotions which issue from a divine source and
inspire him with an innate tendency to behave
morally, is exemplified above all by true love
and friendship. Don Karlos asserts that the
Queen has been granted to him by "heaven and nature"("Mir zuerkannt von Himmel und Natur",673).
What is implied here is that the natural emotion
of love, being a pure and unselfish emotion, is
justified by its very nature; and that there is
a divine order which grants its sanction to such
love. Similarly Don Karlos regards his friendship with Posa as arising from an inborn affin-
ity brought about by "creative nature", an af-
finity which is made manifest by those shared
emotions which mean more to them than all the
world.
Wenn's wahr ist, daß die schaffende Natur
Den Roderich im Karlos wiederholte,
Und unsrer Seelen zartes Saitenspiel
Am Morgen unsres Lebens gleich bezog,
Wenn eine Träne, die mir Lindrung gibt,
Dir teurer ist, als meines Vaters Gnade -
Marquis: O teurer als die ganze Welt.(197ff.)
In the Letters too Schiller is at pains to ex-
plain the contribution made by pure nature to

the idealism of the play; for instance in the
4th Letter he shows how idealism is kindled into
life by the great friendship between Posa and
Don Karlos. "Here is love of a particular person, without neglect of love in general– careful
cultivation of friendship, without the unreason-
ableness, the exclusiveness of this passion.Here
general, all-embracing love of man, concentrated
in a single ray of light. Can that have harmed
the (personal) interest which it has ennobled?
This portrait of friendship – must it necessarily lose in feeling and charm,what it has gained
in compass?"

"Hier ist also Liebe zu einem Wesen, ohne
Hintansetzung der allgemeinen – sorgsame Pflege
der Freundschaft, ohne das Unbillige, das Aus-
schließende dieser Leidenschaft.Hier allgemeine,
alles umfassende Philanthropie,in einen einzigen
Feuerstrahl zusammengedrängt.Und sollte eben das
dem Interesse geschadet haben, was es veredelt
hat? Dieses Gemälde von Freundschaft sollte an
Rührung und Anmut verlieren,was es an Umfang ge-
wann? (NA.22.152)

Thus the union of man's moral or ideal being and his natural self, a union celebrated in
Schiller's "Über Anmut und Würde", is illustrated by Posa's attempt to raise friendship to the
level of idealism, without impairing natural
feeling, the pure nature of friendship.

In contradistinction to the occasional conflict between friendship and love on the one
hand and idealism on the other, a conflict sometimes requiring the former to be sacrificed to
the latter, the more characteristic relation is
that of a close association in which either
friendship or love supplies the inspiration for
idealism. There may be complaints from time to
time that friendship or love is being sacrificed
to idealism, but it is essential that the ideal
itself should not be sacrificed ("Flandern darf/
Nicht aufgeopfert werden", 3458f.).

Posa is not the only idealist, for Don Karlos and the Queen share the same ideals as those
for which he strives. Don Karlos is described by
Posa as a lion-hearted young man to whom the
heroic people of Flanders look for deliverance
(153-4). The Queen shares Don Karlos' enthusiasm
for political reform, as their enemy Domingo is
well aware (2040ff.). When Posa divulges to the
Queen the plan by which Don Karlos is to go to
Flanders to lead a rebellion against Spain, she
becomes more and more enthusiastic, promising
help from France and Savoy (3494-6). Posa himself gives noble expression to the part played
by friendship in inspiring him with his idealistic vision. The friendship which he feels for a
particular person stimulates his heart to beat
for humanity in general. "My heart",he declares,
"dedicated only to a single person, embraced the
whole world! In the soul of my Karlos I created
a paradise for millions."
                    Mein Herz,
        Nur einem einzigen geweiht, umschloß
        Die ganze Welt!- In meines Karlos Seele
        Schuf ich ein Paradies für Millionen.(4257ff)
As he awaits his death Posa asks the Queen to
urge Don Karlos to "make true the bold vision of
a new State, the divine birth of friendship".
                    Er mache-
        O, sagen Sie es ihm! das Traumbild wahr,
        Das kühne Traumbild eines neuen Staates,
        Der Freundschaft göttliche Geburt.(4278-81)
Later Posa explains to Don Karlos, who will sur-
vive him, that he is to dedicate himself to the
task of bringing into being a free Flanders; the
new kingdom is to be his vocation, while Posa's
vocation is to die for Don Karlos (4718-20).The
voluntary act by which Posa sacrifices himself
to the cause of liberty and humanity contrasts
with the involuntary sacrifices which the King
and the Grand Inquisitor exact from their oppressed subjects.

The part played by love in inspiring Don
Karlos with idealism is if anything more important than the influence of friendship, and it illustrates the thin partition that separates two
related processes: the transcending of love as
a spontaneous raising of emotion to the level of
idealism, and on the other hand the regrettable
sacrifice of emotion to a level of idealism regarded almost as inhumanly sublime. In Act 4 the
Queen criticises Posa's decision to sacrifice
his life on the ground that it is an expression
of his pride; it is a decision which she says he
is determined to carry out "even if a thousand
hearts should break".

Mögen tausend Herzen brechen,
Was kümmert Sie's,wenn sich Ihr Stolz nur
weidet. (4385f.)

This contrasts with the Queen's own attempt at
the beginning of the play to inspire Don Karlos
with the thought of an idealism so great that it
would cause his heart to break.

O Karl! Wie groß wird unsre Tugend,
Wenn unser Herz bei ihrer Übung bricht! (768)

Don Karlos' love is not rejected: it is simply
that it must be directed, not to the Queen, but
to the kingdoms that he will one day rule over.

Die Liebe ist Ihr großes Amt. Bis jetzt
Verirrte sie zur Mutter.-Bringen Sie,
O bringen Sie sie Ihren künft'gen Reichen,
Und fühlen Sie, statt Dolchen des Gewissens,
Die Wollust, Gott zu sein. (788-792)

In this passage there is no talk of the "sacrifice" of personal emotion that is sometimes felt
to be involved in idealism. On the contrary, because the Prince's heart belongs properly to his
future subjects, or to humanity in general, he
would be guilty of "wasting" or "sacrificing" it
if he reserved it for a single person,the Queen.

Die Liebe,
Das Herz, das Sie verschwenderisch mir
opfern,

Gehört den Reichen an, die Sie dereinst
Regieren sollen. (783-6)
Thus it is on her own initiative that the Queen
first attempts to raise Don Karlos' love to the
level of idealism, before she is urged to do so
by Posa. Since it is the Queen's wish that the
Prince should interest himself in the fate of
Flanders (901), he attempts, though unsuccessfully, to persuade the King to appoint him Governor of Flanders, in place of Alba. Posa then
conceives the idea of sending Don Karlos to
Flanders as the leader of a rebellion against
Spanish rule, and in accordance with the principle that love should be used to inspire him with
the requisite idealistic zeal, he is to hear the
plan from the lips of the Queen (2453). As we
have seen, the Queen supports the plan, but owing to Posa's misguided decision to work through
the King, nothing comes of the scheme, until Posa can think of no better way of disentangling
himself from his disastrous intrigues and of
saving the Prince's life, than that of sacrificing his own life. Since Posa is doomed, love alone can now provide the inspiration for idealism; it is to the heart of the Queen that Posa
entrusts the task of guiding Don Karlos; it is
upon that sacred altar that he deposits his last
precious testament (4265-8). The Queen faithfully acts in accordance with Posa's wishes, explaining to Don Karlos that Posa died for him
and for the idealistic mission entrusted to him;
Don Karlos duly responds by committing himself
to the aim of creating an ideal political community, a "paradise" that is to arise from Posa's
ashes ("Über seiner Asche blühe/Ein Paradies!",
5296). Don Karlos explains to the Queen that he
has passed the stage at which he could have a
personal love-relation with her. He once loved
her in a personal sense, but now he has "awakened", that is to idealism, to the ideals of
freedom and humanity for which he will fight.

Ich liebte- Jetzt bin ich erwacht. (5312)
The Queen, he says, need no longer fear an out-
break of uncontrolled passion on his part, because a "pure fire", the fire of idealism, has
"purged his being".

                                    Fürchten
Sie keine Wallung mehr von mir. Es ist
Vorbei. Ein reiner Feuer hat mein Wesen
Geläutert.   (5314-7)

So, as Don Karlos declares his determination to
"rescue his oppressed people from the hands of
the tyrant", the Queen can only hide her tears
and express her admiration for a talent which it
is given to man to exercise, but with which wom-
en are less frequently endowed, that of rising
from love to idealism.

                  Ich darf mich nicht
Empor zu dieser Männergröße wagen;
Doch fassen und bewundern kann ich sie.(5349)

     The function of pure nature in inspiring
the pure friend or lover with idealism is illustrated negatively when Don Karlos falls below
the level of pure or idealistic love. We have
seen that he has been preserved from the cor-
rupting influence of the court by his own pure
nature, and this is confirmed in the text of the
play when Domingo admits that it is in vain that
he has tried to corrupt him.

Umsonst versucht' ich's, diesen trotz'gen Mut
In dieser Zeiten Wollust abzumatten.(2035)

But when his love of the Queen acquires an ob-
sessive quality, so that he becomes blind to
idealism and thinks only of enjoying the personal presence of the Queen, then he has fallen
below the level of pure nature. In 2.5. his duel
with Alba symbolises his idealistic opposition
to the authoritarian system prevailing in Spanish territories, but at the appearance of the
Queen, he lowers his sword, kisses the Duke, and
falls at the feet of the Queen. Again, when he
is given a letter which shows that the King is

involved in an intrigue with Princess Eboli, his
one thought is that the Queen is thereby freed
from any obligation to the King,and he is therefore immune to the shock that the news would
otherwise have given to his "strict virtue", as
Princess Eboli puts it.

> Wie kam es,
> Daß seine strenge Tugend hier verstummte?
> (1901f.)

Posa's action in tearing up the letter and in
roundly condemning Don Karlos' passion for the
Queen, has been interpreted as an example of
that high-handed behaviour of which we see more
after he has been appointed to be the King's
Minister. But an examination of the speech in
which he criticises Don Karlos suggests a different interpretation.

> Ja einst,
> Einst war's ganz anders.Da warst du so reich,
> So warm, so reich! Ein ganzer Weltkreis hatte
> In deinem weiten Busen Raum. Das alles
> Ist nun dahin, von einer Leidenschaft,
> Von einem kleinen Eigennutz verschlungen.
> Dein Herz ist ausgestorben. Keine Träne
> Dem ungeheuern Schicksal der Provinzen...
> (2413)

If his love is condemned as an infatuation which
makes him indifferent to the fate of the Provin-
ces, that is more or less what his love has become at this particular stage. Indeed is not his
love similarly dissociated from his idealism at
the beginning of the play? Has not his "sick"
heart ceased to beat for humanity? Are not the
idealistic dreams that he once shared with Posa
a thing of the past ("Vorbei/Sind diese Träume",
178f.)?

We must not be confused by a passage where
Don Karlos tells the King that he and Posa were
joined together by a "nobler bond" than nature
itself could forge("Brüder durch/Ein edler Band,
als die Natur es schmiedet",4793).

Here the word "nature" is used in the more
limited sense of a blood-relationship, the assumption being that people related by blood
should naturally feel affection for each other.
The remark is explained by a passage preceding
it. When the grandees, concerned because Don
Karlos expresses hostility to his father on account of the shooting of his friend Posa, crowd
round to protect the King, the latter appeals to
the principle of nature.

Sind wir

Nicht Sohn und Vater? Ich will doch erwarten,
Zu welcher Schandtat die Natur - (4763-5)
But Don Karlos interrupts him to say that the
murder of Posa has destroyed any natural affection he once felt for his father.

Natur?

Ich weiß von keiner.Mord ist jetzt die

Losung.

Der Menschheit Bande sind entzwei.
In another passage Don Karlos similarly declares
that nature has died out in his heart ("Ausge-
storben ist/In meinem Busen die Natur", 5341f.).
It is a mistake to give to the two references to
nature in these passages any far-reaching significance, or to ask how Don Karlos, in his plan
to liberate Flanders, can act on the principle
of nature bequeathed to him by Posa, if all natural feeling has died out in him. The last passage is immediately preceded by a reference to
his father whom he can no longer love, because
he has killed his dearest friend. We must judge
such references to nature in the light of the
circumstances in which they are made. Of course
it is possible for Don Karlos to disown all natural affection for his father, while at the same
time continuing to affirm the natural humanity
which he feels for the people of Flanders, whom
he hopes to liberate.

There is therefore adequate evidence of the
important part played by nature in the work, a

principle in accordance with which Posa not only
expands his personal friendship with Don Karlos
to idealistic love of humanity in general, but
also encourages the Queen and the Prince to en-
noble their love in much the same way.The critic
is right to stress the fact that Posa through
his "Schwärmerei" or fanaticism, is guilty of
betraying his own idealism; but if he fails to
bring out the important contribution which the
principle of nature, despite Posa's aberration,
is nevertheless able to make to the cause of idealism, he is scarcely giving a faithful account
of the work. Idealism and pure nature are natural allies. It is as misleading to maintain that
Schiller in this play repudiates idealism, as it
is to suppress the part played by nature, or to
replace it with another philosophy, that of existentialism, which if it had been present in
the play, would have been opposed to idealism.

Posa not only deserves credit for understanding that friendship and love, by their in-
herent purity, serve to inspire the person concerned with idealistic aspiration. There are
other ways in which he acts as an advocate of
nature regarded as a principle opposed to the
false doctrine of despotism upheld by King Philipp and the Grand Inquisitor.

Despite, or perhaps on account of the outward power which the King wields with such absolute authority, inwardly his morale is under-
mined by loneliness, by lack of friendship, by
a dearth of natural feeling. In his audience
with the King in 3.10. Posa appeals to him in
the name of pure nature, of that inner life of
the soul in which he is impoverished. Don Karlos, in his audience with the King in 2.2., has
already anticipated the appeal which Posa makes.
"How delightful and sweet it is to feel exalted
in a beautiful soul", he tells the King; "to
behold our joy reflected in our friend's eyes,to
know that our fear causes his heart to tremble,
and that our sorrows bring tears to his eyes!"

In 3.5. the King prays that he may be given a "human being" who, unlike his other court advisers, can be relied upon to speak the truth to him and advise him without thought of self-interest. But in the version of 1805 he asks, not only for someone to advise him, but also for a "friend", a request that is not included in the 1787 version.

Ich bitte dich um einen Freund... (2813)

The King is concerned, not only with problems of State, but also with his own personal problems. It is to the King's personal need for friendship that Posa addresses himself in his actual audience. He points out that, although the King has set himself up as an absolute monarch, as a kind of God, nevertheless he remains a human being with a human being's sensitivity and need for sympathy (3113-6).

We have seen the numerous ways in which the image of the "sacrifice" has been employed in the play; and in Posa's audience with the King we are reminded of the Flemings who have been sacrificed (3146-8). But perhaps the most telling use of this image is Posa's reference to the King as a person who, although he is in need of human sympathy, confronts his subjects as a kind of God, to whom they can only offer up sacrifice, or before whom they must stand trembling and praying.

Sie brauchen Mitgefühl - und einem Gott
Kann man nur opfern - zittern - zu ihm beten!
(3116f.)

The relationship in which one of two persons can only offer up a sacrifice to the other, is seen, not simply as a violation of human right, but as a "perversion of nature", because it precludes those pure natural emotions which should be experienced in a human relation.

Bereuenswerter Tausch! Unselige
Verdrehung der Natur! (3118)

It is not only the person making the "sacrifice"

who suffers from this "perversion of nature",
but in an even more bitterly ironic sense the
King himself, who has to accept a hollow obeis-
ance in place of the true expression of friendship for which his heart yearns.

In the Hamburg stage-version of 1787 the
"perversion of nature" is expressed rather more
poignantly. "They do not dare to feel (in sympathy) with him. However loudly, however urgent-
ly suffering nature calls from their heart."

Mit ihm zu fühlen wagt man nicht. So laut,
so dringend auch die leidende Natur
hervor aus ihrem Busen ruft.(2116-8)

It is not in vain that Posa appeals to the despot's need for a friend, as is shown by the
King's exclamation:"Bei Gott,/Er greift in meine
Seele!" (3121).By making this appeal, Posa aims
at enabling the King to come to a better understanding of human nature, to appreciate the pure
nature, the natural morality that is its essential principle.

The conflict in the play is not simply between the despotism of King Philipp and the ideal of freedom advanced by Posa: it is a conflict between an abstract system of morality imposed on the people by the absolute authority of
the State and the Church on the one hand, and on
the other the pure nature, the moral instinct
with which man has been endowed, an instinct
which enables him to do what is morally right by
his own spontaneous impulse.

It is not only of freedom that Posa speaks
in his audience with the King; he also speaks of
morality, to which he refers in terms of "human
dignity" ("Menschenwürde", 3092), "nobility"
("Adel", 3097), man's "inner greatness" ("innere
Größe", 3100), or the "sublime, proud virtues of
freedom"("der Freiheit erhabne,stolze Tugenden",
3248-9). At first, because the King has been ac-
customed only to the flattery of his courtiers,
he does not recognise the "human dignity" or the

inner integrity of a free man like Posa.
              Ich höre, Sire, wie klein,
Wie niedrig Sie von Menschenwürde denken,
Selbst in des freien Mannes Sprache nur
Den Kunstgriff eines Schmeichlers sehen...
                      (3091-4)
The courtiers themselves have forfeited their
inner "nobility", have fled from the spectre of
their "inner greatness".
              ...die haben
Freiwillig ihres Adels sich begeben,
Freiwillig sich auf diese niedre Stufe
Herab gestellt. Erschrocken fliehen Sie
Vor dem Gespenste ihrer innern Größe.(3096)
    We have seen that Posa vindicates the prin-
ciple of nature by demonstrating that the pure
emotions of the human heart serve to inspire man
with his idealism;and by appealing to the King's
personal need of natural affection, he demonstrates the vital part played by pure nature in
human existence. But in his representations to
the King another belief finds expression: that
the pure emotions which enable man to do what is
morally right originate in a divine source from
which they derive their validation. Spontaneous
the pure emotions of the human heart may be, but
they are not capricious. The principles by which
men, influenced by their pure emotions, feel im-
pelled to act, are as firm, as absolute as those
of any despot, indeed more so. They are absolute, not as the decrees of a despot are absolute, not in the sense that they are imposed by
the King on his subjects unconditionally. The
principles of pure nature are absolute in the
sense that they issue from God himself, who has
made men such that they naturally desire to
follow His laws, so long as they act on their
pure emotions.
    Posa's appeal to the King is supported by
his underlying belief that man's pure nature is
an expression of a moral order against which no

artificial despotism can prevail. The image of
the "sacrifice" is introduced yet again, when
Posa tells the King that his "struggle with nature" has been in vain, and that he has "sacrificed" his life to projects which were "destructive", meaning that they were intended to destroy natural morality.

Dem Undank haben Sie gebaut - umsonst
Den harten Kampf mit der Natur gerungen,
Umsonst ein großes königliches Leben
Zerstörenden Entwürfen hingeopfert.(3184-7)

Posa's faith in the inevitable triumph of the
moral order associated with the principle of nature, is seen in his reference to the futility
of the King's attempt to hold up the new spring-
time of the human spirit.

Und Sie hoffen...
Den allgemeinen Frühling aufzuhalten,
Der die Gestalt der Welt verjüngt? (3162-6)

Audacious though Posa's demand may appear, that
the King should renounce, as he says, the "unnatural deification" of the absolute ruler -

Geben Sie
Die unnatürliche Vergött'rung auf,
Die uns vernichtet. Werden Sie unser Muster
Des Ewigen und Wahren. (3206-9)

- we must understand that in Posa's belief the
moral order, to which he refers here as the
"Eternal and the True",is incomparably more powerful than any petty despotism invented by man.
But if the King cannot prevail against the eternal moral order, Posa suggests that he could
find a worthy rôle for himself by serving the
moral order, by becoming so to speak its model
or representative. When Posa refers to the fact
that the King cannot but "tremble at every virtue",he means that the individual's pure nature,
drawing its strength from God, represents an independent moral authority for which the King's
worldly power is no match.

Sie müssen
Vor jeder Tugend zittern. (3225)

In hoping that the King, the embodiment of ab-
solutism, might become an exemplar of pure nature, Posa shows that he is looking for the complete conversion of the King almost in a religious sense: a conversion which might well transform the world.
Ein Federzug von dieser Hand, und neu
Erschaffen wird die Welt. (3214)
At first sight there appears to be a contradiction between the picture which Posa has already
drawn of the King's vain attempt to contend with
nature and to hold up the fulfilment of man's
true destiny, and on the other hand the transformation which the King is now represented as
capable of bringing about by granting freedom of
thought ("Geben Sie/Gedankenfreiheit", 3215).
But by removing the external constraint the King
can provide the necessary conditions for man's
pure humanity to develop, or as Posa expresses
the matter, he can restore the lost "nobility"
of mankind ("Stellen Sie der Menschheit/Verlor-
nen Adel wieder her", 3242). The positive bene-
fit which would result from the conversion of
the King would not be anything which he could
directly give; but freedom would enable man, as
Posa says, to be restored to himself, restored
to his "lost nobility", his own pure nature; for
man's inner "virtue" or natural morality can
thrive only if its spontaneity or freedom is not
impaired.
Wenn nun der Mensch,sich selbst zurückgegeben,
Zu seines Werts Gefühl erwacht – der Freiheit
Erhabne, stolze Tugenden gedeihen... (3247-9)
        Idealism,far from being discredited in this
play, either by Posa's lapse into "Schwärmerei"
or by the failure of his plans in this particular case,is vindicated by the moral victory that
it wins. The momentum of the King's public life
obliges him to go on playing the same authoritarian rôle as before, but his private self has
been transformed by his audience with Posa.

Ich hab' ihn liebgehabt, sehr lieb. Er war
Mir teuer wie mein Sohn. In diesem Jüngling
Ging mir ein neuer, schönrer Morgen auf.(5050)
Even in death, as Alba complains, Posa steals
the King's heart from his courtiers (5047); for
they are as nothing compared to the "one free
man who stood up in the whole century".
Ein freier Mann stand auf in diesem ganzen
Jahrhundert.   (5044)
The King appreciates the fact that Posa's heart
"beat for all humanity".
                 Der Freundschaft arme Flamme
Füllt eines Posa Herz nicht aus. Das schlug
Der ganzen Menschheit.   (5060-2)
It is true that the King, stung by the thought
that Posa passed him over in favour of his son,
resolves to ridicule his idea of "virtue", that
is his idealism, his belief in natural morality.
                 Ich will
Ihn zum Gelächter machen. Seine Tugend
Sei eines Träumers Hirngespinst gewesen.(5077)
But in general that does not truly represent his
response to Posa's ideas. Perhaps the greatest
tribute to Posa's success in winning the King
over to his views, is paid by his bitterest enemy, the Grand Inquisitor. "Where at that time
was the Philipp whose firm soul, like the pole
star in the sky, revolved everlastingly about
itself, without changing? Had a whole past age
receded behind you? At that moment when you
offered him your hand, was the world no longer
the same? Poison no longer poison? The partition
between good and evil, and true and false, had
it fallen?"
                 War zwischen Gut und Übel
Und Wahr und Falsch die Scheidewand gefallen?
      (5203)
But the Grand Inquisitor is mistaken. The partition is still there: it is the concept of good
and evil that has changed. One kind of absolute
authority,the political authority of the despot,

is discredited; and on the other side of the
partition is the absolute authority of a moral
order that works through pure nature or natural
morality.

Far from replacing idealism with an amoral
existentialist creed,Schiller reinforces it with
a nature-philosophy imbued with a moralism entirely in accord with idealism.There is no place
in this work for an existentialist philosophy
wholly alien to Schiller.

Nor is the existentially minded critic justified in extracting any moral support from
Schiller's comparison of the types of the idealist and the realist in the concluding part of
his "Über naive und sentimentalische Dichtung".
Schiller's point is not that the realist is to
be preferred to the idealist (K.H.39), but that
in view of the "one-sidedness" of both systems
("die Einseitigkeit beider Systeme", NA.20.499),
the ideal of human nature is fully attained by
neither in isolation, but only by combining the
two ("daß das Ideal menschlicher Natur unter
beide verteilt, von keinem aber völlig erreicht
ist", NA.20.500). Furthermore Schiller in this
passage associates realism with the process of
cultivating man as a creature of nature, which
process he regards as the necessary condition
for all "moral ennoblement".

Aber der Idealist für sich allein würde eben-
sowenig die sinnlichen Kräfte kultiviert und
den Menschen als Naturwesen ausgebildet haben,
welches doch...die Bedingung aller moralischen Veredlung ist.   (NA.20.499)

This is the philosophy of pure nature which we
have seen operating in "Don Karlos", a nature-
philosophy which, far from opposing idealism,
supports it with the "moral ennoblement" which
it provides. Thus Schiller's concept of realism
scarcely supplies any assistance to the critic
with an existentialist axe to grind.

CHAPTER FOUR

WALLENSTEIN

In any interpretation of "Wallenstein" the critic must make clear his views on certain key questions raised by the play. What importance is to be attached to the view that conflict between Wallenstein and the Emperor is largely brought about by mutual suspicion, and by defensive arrangements made by each side against the other? Is Wallenstein justified in claiming that the Emperor has forfeited his legitimacy as Emperor? Has Wallenstein any legitimate right to usurp the authority of the Emperor?

Our views on these questions are as follows. Mutual suspicion plays only a limited part in bringing about the conflict. The suspicion arises in the first place from actions taken by one side against the other; the Emperor's suspicion can be traced back to Wallenstein's high-handed action in making himself an independent power in the land. The argument that Wallenstein does no more than to defend himself against precautions taken against him by the Emperor, is fallacious; the Emperor's precautions have been necessitated by Wallenstein's earlier actions.

The legitimacy of the Emperor, as the representative of a moral order, is not affected by Wallenstein's claim that he acts only in his own interest, and not for the good of the whole of society. We have only Wallenstein's subjective assertion, and nothing like an objective statement in the play that the Emperor is unworthy of his position.

Thirdly our view is that Wallenstein is not justified in attempting to usurp the authority of the Emperor, since he is motivated merely by ambition, and has no idealism, no moral vision

which would justify him in making the attempt.
He is portrayed as a great man in the sense that
he has great ability as a military commander,
and inspires his men with confidence. But he is
also portrayed as above all an ambitious man,who
thinks of himself as engaged in a power-struggle
in which moral considerations play scarcely any
part. Moral issues only complicate the kind of
straightforward contest of force against force
which he prefers (W.T.200.ff). The imperial army
which Wallenstein has forged is the weapon by
which he seeks to fulfil his ambition. Questenberg describes this army as an unreliable force
led by an unreliable commander,a fearful instrument entrusted in blind obedience to the most
arrogant of men.

Und die Armee, von der wir Hilf erwarten,
. . . .
Vom Schwindelnden die schwindelnde geführt,
Ein furchtbar Werkzeug, dem verwegensten
Der Menschen blind gehorchend hingegeben.P.325

If the opinion of Questenberg, one of the Emper-
or's men, is regarded as biased, the same testi-
mony is forthcoming from within Wallenstein's
own camp. It is as though Wallenstein had not
received his command from the Emperor; he has
used his power, not for the good of his country,
but in order to establish a military empire.

Der führt's Kommando nicht wie ein Amt,
Wie eine Gewalt, die vom Kaiser stammt!
Es ist ihm nicht um des Kaisers Dienst,
Was bracht er dem Kaiser für Gewinst?
Was hat er mit seiner großen Macht
Zu des Landes Schirm und Schutz vollbracht?
Ein Reich von Soldaten wollt er gründen.L.326.

His assumption of independent authority is high-
lighted by the fact that he even arranges for
the minting of his own coinage (L.871.ff.).

Foremost among the specious arguments Wallenstein produces is the claim that, since the
Emperor intends to dismiss him, he has a right

to forestall the Emperor.
Der Hof hat meinen Untergang beschlossen,
Drum bin ich willens, ihm zuvor zu kommen.
(W.T.705f.)
The Gräfin herself puts forward the same argu-
ment, appealing to Wallenstein's right of self-
defence ("Notwehr",W.T.548). Wallenstein thinks
of dismissal as tantamount to "force", which he
proposes to anticipate by using force himself.
Ich muß Gewalt ausüben oder leiden.(W.T.766)
He claims that he is simply obeying the law of
the stronger, according to which, to avoid being
vanquished, he must vanquish his opponent.
Wer nicht vertrieben sein will,muß vertreiben,
Da herrscht der Streit, und nur die Stärke
siegt. (W.T.791f.)
All three quotations in which Wallenstein speaks
of retaliating against the Emperor, are based on
the unspoken assumption that he is justified in
claiming equality with the Emperor, that he is
on a level with his master.It cannot be accepted
that the head of State has no right to dismiss
an army commander; nor is an army commander,when
dismissed, entitled to subvert the authority of
the Emperor who has dismissed him.
      Schiller's well-known pronouncement on Wal-
lenstein at the end of Book IV of his History of
the Thirty Years' War - "Wallenstein fell, not
because he was a rebel, but he became a rebel
because he fell" - is unsatisfactory, because
one must trace the cause of Wallenstein's rebellion, not just to his dismissal or "fall"
from office, but further back to the cause of
his dismissal. Nor is the passage rendered any
more satisfactory by the preceding sentence. "If
necessity and despair at last forced him to deserve the sentence which had been pronounced against him while innocent, still this, if true,
will not justify that sentence" (A.J.W.M.p.293).
Innocent? This eleventh-hour attempt to excuse
Wallenstein contradicts Schiller's own account

earlier in the work."His armies flourished while
all the States through which they passed with-
ered. What cared he for the detestation of the
people?...His armies adored him...His design un-
questionably was that his sovereign should stand
in fear...beside him. The terrified Emperor was
assailed on all sides by petitions against Wallenstein, and his ear filled with the most fearful descriptions of his outrages" (ibid.105 and
113). Nor is the portrait of Wallenstein in the
play itself any better; for in the "Lager" it is
the portrait of a commander who permits licence
and immorality (L.223). The association of Wallenstein's name with the kind of freedom that is
based on "might" tells the same story.
Freiheit ist bei der Macht allein,
Ich leb und sterb bei dem Wallenstein.(L.1023)
It is not the case that Wallenstein "rebelled"
because he was dismissed at Regensburg; long before that, he was lawless and irresponsible, as
well as disloyal to the Emperor, who had good
reasons for dismissing him. Indeed, contrary to
what is sometimes suggested, the Emperor's action in dismissing Wallenstein redounds greatly
to his credit as the defender of a moral order
which Wallenstein endangers with his ambition
and lawlessness.

Opposed to Wallenstein as the representative
of the imperial cause is Octavio Piccolomini,
whose belief in a moral order emerges clearly in
the debate that he has with Max in P.1.4. The
remarkable suggestion has been made that the
concept of a moral order is discredited at the
outset by the fact that it is associated with
whatever is "krumm", that is crooked, devious or
dishonest (H.H.321). Let us examine the passage.
According to Max, Wallenstein finds his inspiration within himself and is unwilling to be guided by instructions laid down for him.He consults
the "living oracle" in his inner self, not old
orders or mouldy papers.

Das Orakel
In seinem Innern, das lebendige, –
Nicht tote Bücher, alte Ordnungen,
Nicht modrigte Papiere soll er fragen.(P.459)
In the narrower sense Max is discussing Wallen-
stein as a military commander, but the reference
to the inner "oracle" extends the discussion to
Wallenstein's outlook on life in general.Octavio
for his part takes Max's distinction between
"living oracle" and "old orders" in the widest
possible sense, as referring to two contrasted
ways of life.
Mein Sohn! Laß uns die alten, engen Ordnungen
Gering nicht achten!....
Denn immer war die Willkür fürchterlich –
Der Weg der Ordnung,ging er auch durch
                              Krümmen,
Er ist kein Umweg.   (P.463-9)
The "old orders" referred to by Max have now
been transmuted into the principle of "order"
itself, which Octavio commends in preference to
"Willkür" – the wilful, arbitrary, lawless ten-
dency which Octavio, putting his own construc-
tion on the "inner oracle", attributes to Wal-
lenstein. The distinction between "Willkür" and
"Ordnung" is next described in terms of movement
in a straight line contrasted with a winding or
circuitous movement (for instance the path of a
road or the course of a river).
Der Weg der Ordnung, ging er auch durch
                              Krümmen,
Er ist kein Umweg.Grad aus geht des Blitzes,
Geht des Kanonballs fürchterlicher Pfad –
....
Mein Sohn!Die Straße,die der Mensch befährt,
Worauf der Segen wandelt, diese folgt
Der Flüsse Lauf, der Täler freien Krümmen,
Umgeht das Weizenfeld, den Rebenhügel,
Des Eigentums gemeßne Grenzen ehrend –
So führt sie später, sicher doch zum Ziel.
                    (P.468ff.)

An object moving in a straight line (for instance a cannonball or a flash of lightning) is
opposed to the principle of order, because it
collides with anything in its path, and is hence
destructive. On the other hand an object describing a circuitous movement acts in accordance
with the principle of order, since it takes account of whatever lies in its path; a field of
wheat or a vineyard on a hillside is bypassed,
and the measured boundaries of property are respected. Thus Octavio associates Wallenstein's
"inner oracle" with the arbitrary unyielding
path of destruction; but the circuitous path
which yields to the rights of others, is the
path on which man's blessing is to be found, the
path of "order".

The kind of "straightforward" and destructive movement referred to in this passage, is exemplified in the "Lager", 213–223, by the description of the movement of Wallenstein's "wild"
army, as they go on their destructive way across
country and "through the crops and the yellow
corn", putting an end to "order" and discipline.

Wir heißen des Friedländers wilde Jagd,
. . . .
Ziehen frech durch Feindes und Freundes Lande,
Querfeldein durch die Saat,durch das gelbe
                                    Korn –
. . . .
Keine Ordnung gilt mehr und keine Zucht.

We see therefore that the "path of order" is associated, not with what is "crooked" or devious
in a pejorative sense, but with the avoidance of
any action that would infringe the rights of
others. The meanings of the symbolic expressions
"krumm" and "gerade" are not "deceit" and "honesty" respectively, as has been suggested, but
on the contrary respect for order and the rights
of others in the case of "krumm", and arbitrary
action or even lawlessness and violence in the
case of "gerade". It is not that the concept of

"order" is discredited by association with what
is "crooked"; on the contrary the idea of taking
a roundabout course is used to illustrate respect for the rights of others and hence for the
principle of "order".

Octavio's concept of "order" is humane and
civilised; it has nothing to do with the authoritarian imposition of order from above, but is
based simply on the moral principle of consider-
ing the rights of one's fellow beings.

It is only in subsequent passages where
these expressions are used that they come to
refer to deceit in the case of "krumm", and honesty in the case of "gerade". As the characters
who claim that they are "straightforward" or
honest, or who deny that they are "crooked" or
dishonest, are rarely justified in making their
claim or denial, there is usually a certain irony attaching to their remarks. When Max claims
that Wallenstein "hates crooked ways" ("Er...
haßt die krummen Wege",P.1701), we think of Wallenstein's secret intrigues with the Swedes against the Emperor. Max disagrees with the part
played by Octavio in spying on Wallenstein in
order to counteract his betrayal of the Emperor,
and declares that his own course must be honest
or straightforward ("Mein Weg muß gerad sein",
P.2603). He makes the same point later ("Dein
Weg ist krumm,er ist der meine nicht",W.T.1192).
But when Max threatens to go to Wallenstein and
to challenge him to defend his reputation, tearing apart Octavio's web of intrigue in his own
characteristically "straightforward" manner -
Ich geh zum Herzog.Heut noch werd ich ihn
Auffordern,seinen Leumund vor der Welt
Zu retten, eure künstlichen Gewebe
Mit einem graden Schritte zu durchreißen.
                    (P.2610)
- it occurs to us (and Octavio himself virtually
makes this very point) that Max's straightforward action in speaking openly to Wallenstein,

would be "gerad" in the sense originally indicated by Octavio, since it would be arbitrary
action likely to endanger the moral order defended by the Emperor. Again, when Buttler is
asked to sign the Pilsen Resolution, he parades
his virtue by making it known that he will support Wallenstein out of conviction, not because
the trick devised by those who have drawn up the
Resolution will "bend his straightforward judgment" ("Ihr werdet...nicht erwarten,/Daß euer
Spiel mein grades Urteil krümmt", P.1986). His
judgment is not so "straightforward" in the
sense of "honest", that it will not later be
sufficiently deflected to let him act straight-
forwardly in Octavio's sense of "arbitrarily" or
"lawlessly", by assassinating Wallenstein.

When at last Wallenstein is made to realise
that Octavio has been spying on him to counteract his plans to betray the Emperor, he denoun-
ces Octavio's "wicked heart", contrasting it
with his own "straightforward" or honest heart.
Dein schlechtes Herz hat über mein gerades
Den schändlichen Triumph davon getragen.
                    (W.T.1683f.)
In view of Wallenstein's own intrigues against
the Emperor, the irony is obvious.

We must not be confused by Max's defence of
Wallenstein, or by the fact that he accuses Octavio himself of adopting "crooked" ways. Wallenstein is crooked or devious in promoting his
own interests at the expense of society as a
whole. Octavio is crooked or devious in protect-
ing society from the effects of Wallenstein's
ambition.

In the early part of the play Max is completely mistaken in his judgment of Wallenstein.
His deep feeling of friendship prevents him from
believing that Wallenstein would betray the Emperor. Max, as a sensitive person, in fact a
"beautiful soul", has been much moved by a jour-
ney which he has made through countries living

in peace. He has a vision of life in all its
beauty, a land so to speak which the army, like
a band of robbers, has merely skirted round.
Army life leaves his heart in a barren condition
(P.524); warfare is too negative to offer any
satisfaction to his soul (P.531). His longing
for peace really puts Max on the same side as
his father Octavio;but in his naive hero-worship
he accepts Wallenstein's pretence that he is
working for peace. More genuine is Octavio's belief in an enduring condition of peace ("Das
ruhig, mächtig Dauernde", P.489), contrasting
with the spectacular but destructive events of
wartime. Max's mistaken faith in Wallenstein at
first obscures the fact that he is by nature in
favour of "order" and opposed to lawlessness.

In P.5.1. Octavio reveals to Max the full
extent of Wallenstein's intrigues, describes him
as a lawless figure confronting the State which
it is his duty to protect (P.2351f.), refers to
the deception practised by Wallenstein on his
officers in the matter of the oath of allegiance, and finally shows Max a document signed
by the Emperor, in which he outlaws Wallenstein
and gives Octavio temporary command of the army
(P.2499ff.).

There is irony in Max's assertion that Wallenstein will presently be seen triumphantly em-
erging in his purity from the dark cloud of suspicion in which he is enveloped. Almost immediately Max himself witnesses the arrival of a
messenger who reports that Sesina, while riding
on his way to Regensburg with dispatches from
Wallenstein to the Swedes, has been captured by
the Emperor's men.

In Wallenstein's monologue in W.T.1.4. there
are two main strands of thought, the first of
which is the incalculable nature of events in
the world at large. In the first section (139-
158) his dismay at the capture of Sesina arises
from the fact that it belies his faith in his

ability, by means of astrology, to predict a
favourable time for action; it unsettles his
confidence in his power so to command Fate as to
control the complicated factors of the power-
struggle in which he is engaged. Now the tables
seem to have been turned on him, as though he
were obliged to carry out the deed simply because he has thought it.

His thought of betraying the Emperor was a
mere "dream", he says, it was simply a question
of keeping his options open, no serious or firm
decision had been reached, it was merely a matter of toying with the idea, of enjoying the
sense of being free to take this action if he
wished. This is only partly true; for although
he has not yet committed himself, nevertheless
by dispatching Sesina to the Swedes he has taken
action to that end.

The first strand of thought is not uncon-
nected with the second, which is the immorality
of the action contemplated, that of betraying
the Emperor. Wallenstein's interest in astrology
as a means of calculating the course of events
replaces for him the moral aspect of the matter,
since he does not start by asking what he is
morally obliged to do, but by asking what the
situation permits him to undertake successfully.
This elimination of any tendency to act on principle gives him a false sense of freedom, which
is expressed when he speaks to Terzky of the
pleasure he takes in contemplating the thought
of his power, irrespective of whether he will
use it or not (P.868ff.).

Wallenstein thinks that so long as he does
not positively commit himself to betraying the
Emperor, he is free to negotiate with the Emperor's enemies. But when his envoy is captured
and the thing becomes known, the moral aspect of
the matter is forced upon his attention, because
not only the Emperor, but the people as a whole
consider his action from a moral point of view.

It is his discounting of the moral aspect of the
action he contemplates which, by encouraging him
to go ahead, has trapped him, has caused him to
adopt an immoral stance in the eyes of the
world; suddenly, while he is standing on the
stage, the lights go up and he is revealed as a
traitor, a rôle which he cannot easily shake
off. It was the moral aspect which was missing
from his calculations: it is the moral aspect
which has destroyed his calculations. The two
strands of thought in the monologue are one.

The second strand of thought has already
been introduced in the previous scene, where he
admits that he has been "playing with the devil"
("Verflucht,wer mit dem Teufel spielt!",WT.114).
He even mentions the possibility of returning
"honourably" to his "duty", though it might be
too late to do so.

Und kehr ich noch so ehrlich auch zurück
Zu meiner Pflicht,es wird mir nichts mehr
                helfen - (WT.108f.)

In the first part of the monologue he speaks of
his proposed action against the Emperor as a
"temptation" (WT.142). He also speaks of the
"good way" lying to one side, of which he has
been conscious during his intrigues,and to which
he has assumed that he was free to return.

Und sah ich nicht den guten Weg zur Seite,
Der mir die Rückkehr offen stets bewahrte.
                (WT.153f.)

So Wallenstein agonises over the moral aspect of
his action despite himself.

In the second part of the monologue (159-
179) he thinks, not of his own conscience, but
of his moral standing in the eyes of the world
(a question forced upon him by the capture of
Sesina). To admit his own guilt to himself, is
one thing; but that other people should regard
him as guilty - that is a different matter. He
is now concerned with what he claims to be the
mere appearance of guilt,the fact that suspicion

is apt to poison his "pure deed", so that it
bears no resemblance to the "innocence", the
"uncorrupted will" to which he lays claim.

Strafbar erschein ich, und ich kann die Schuld,
Wie ichs versuchen mag! nicht von mir wälzen;
Denn mich verklagt der Doppelsinn des Lebens,
Und - selbst der frommen Quelle reine Tat
Wird der Verdacht, schlimmdeutend, mir vergiften.

If he had really been a traitor, he argues,
he would have been careful to preserve an appearance of innocence; but since, as he claims,
he was conscious of his innocence, he was not
afraid to give vent on occasion to his feeling
of annoyance or impatience with the Emperor.

Der Unschuld,
Des unverführten Willens mir bewußt,
Gab ich der Laune Raum, der Leidenschaft -

Now his enemies will put an artificial construction on what were really harmless expressions of
feeling, weaving a web of damning evidence against him, which he will not be able to refute.
So through his lack of circumspection he has
fatally ensnared himself in a "net" for which
his own misleading conduct has provided the mat-
erial. It all sounds very convincing, provided
we overlook one thing, which is that in this
part of the monologue he does not refer to the
event which as he knows is likely to give proof
of his treachery, the capture of Sesina. Wallenstein is disingenuous. He claims that he has
sometimes spoken out boldly against the Emperor,
secure in the knowledge that he has not committed any hostile action against him.

Kühn was das Wort, weil es die Tat nicht war.

He says this despite the fact that, through the
capture of Sesina, it will be confirmed that he
has been engaged in treasonable negotiations
with the Swedes, negotiations which according to
Wrangel have been dragging on for over a year.

Ins zweite Jahr schon schleicht die Unter-
                    handlung. (WT.405)

It is in vain that Wallenstein attempts to
exonerate himself by reference to certain harmless expressions of annoyance with the Emperor.
The real "net" with which he has ensnared himself (WT.177f.), is not the net of his unguarded
outbursts against the Emperor, but the net of
his negotiations with the Emperor's enemies.

In introducing the idea of the "ambiguity
of life" ("der Doppelsinn des Lebens", WT.161),
Wallenstein in this particular passage simply
refers to the danger that an innocent person may
give a false impression of guilt; or more spec-
ifically, that he himself, by his expressions of
annoyance, may have given the impression that he
is disloyal to the Emperor. But the fact that he
uses his allegedly ambiguous outbursts of impatience as a red herring to distract attention
from his negotiations with the Emperor's enemies, does not encourage us to give much cred-
ence to the idea of ambiguity, which serves
merely as an excuse at which he grasps in an attempt to maintain his innocence. Although in the
present passage Wallenstein claims that he is
innocent despite his appearance of guilt, his
conduct is in fact "ambiguous" in the opposite
sense: his specious attempt to prove his innocence fails to conceal his guilt. It is his
claim to innocence, not his dubious reputation
that is false. Wallenstein would have us believe
that there is a certain general property of life
which gives men's actions a certain undeserved
ambiguity. It is only a device by which he hopes
to exonerate himself. If Wallenstein is "ambiguous" or perfidious in his relations with the Emperor, this is because he has chosen to be so.
The Pilsen Resolution is ambiguous because Wallenstein permits Illo to make it so.

To explain Wallenstein's phrase about the
"ambiguity of life" by reference to the tendency
of politicians acting on self-interest to appeal
to certain noble principles,and to maintain that

Wallenstein is no worse than his opponents, is to assist him in his work of whitewashing himself. Wallenstein is not a politician: he is a military commander who betrays the cause to which morally and legally he is committed.

We come now to the third section of the monologue (W.T.180-191), containing the reference to "des Lebens Fremde" (189) - the "alien field of life".

In meiner Brust war meine Tat noch mein:
Einmal entlassen aus dem sichern Winkel
Des Herzens, ihrem mütterlichen Boden,
Hinausgegeben in des Lebens Fremde,
Gehört sie jenen tückschen Mächten an,
Die keines Menschen Kunst vertraulich macht.

In my innermost self my "deed", that is my as yet unperformed deed or intention,is still mine; but when it is released from the secure corner of the heart, its maternal ground, and is delivered over to the alien field of life, in what sense is my deed at the mercy of certain malicious powers?

In the first place the passage that leads up to the reference to "des Lebens Fremde" makes it clear that Wallenstein is at least partly referring to the first strand of thought, the discovery that he is no longer in control of the power-game.

Wie anders! da des Mutes freier Trieb
Zur kühnen Tat mich zog, die rauh gebietend
Die Not jetzt, die Erhaltung von mir heischt.
Ernst ist der Anblick der Notwendigkeit.
Nicht ohne Schauder greift des Menschen Hand
In des Geschicks geheimnisvolle Urne.(180-5)

Wallenstein's knowledge of human fate, assisted by astrology, no longer enables him to command Fate, no longer gives him an advantage in the power-struggle. He is as subject to Fate, and to the "necessity" that Fate imposes, as anyone else; and it is not without a shudder of apprehension that he puts his hand in the mysterious

urn of Fate.Once Wallenstein's contemplated deed
has left the "secure corner of the heart" and
entered the "alien field of life", he discovers
that its consequences are far less calculable
than he had hoped, that it exposes him to a number of unexpected hazards.

But there is another sense in which Wallenstein's "deed" is alienated when it is no longer
simply a contemplated deed, but has actually
been carried out; for there is also the moral
aspect of the matter. We have seen that in the
second section Wallenstein maintains that he is
not really guilty. His deed, he claims, is a
"pure" deed arising from a "pious" source, that
is from his moral self("der frommen Quelle reine
Tat",162); he is conscious of his "innocence",
of his "uncorrupted will" ("Der Unschuld,/Des
unverführten Willens mir bewußt",167f.). It is
only that "suspicion" poisons his "pure deed".

Now in the third section Wallenstein attempts to confirm this contrast between what he
claims is the moral purity of his inner self and
the false appearance of guilt that is given to
his deed in the outer world. The reference to
"der sichere Winkel des Herzens" (187) means that
the inner self, the "corner of the heart" is secure, because it produces only innocent or pure
thoughts and intentions. Throughout the play the
"heart" refers either to ideal love or to conscience; it is a moral concept. The suggestion
is that the contemplated deed is falsified once
it has entered the "alien field of life": it is
not the deed itself that is at fault, but the
field in which it expresses itself, the outer
world where it is misjudged, misrepresented. So
Wallenstein tries to shift the blame from himself to the world which condemns him.

A number of writers have associated the
phrase "des Lebens Fremde" with the materialistic aspect of the world. According to one writer:
"Here it is clearly demonstrated that what is

contrary to God prevails in common reality"(K.M.
129). Another critic relates "des Lebens Fremde"
to "das ganz Gemeine", the common or materialistic aspect of life discussed in the next section of the monologue (J.B.406f.). A third associates "des Lebens Fremde" with the process by
which a man's free thought becomes fixed in the
world's rigid structure, and he speaks of Wallenstein as hesitating before the prospect of
being contaminated by the reality of the world
(C.H.228,233).

The reference to the "alien field of life"
conjures up an image of an idealist such as Max
Piccolomini standing over against a hostile materialistic world. Where the critics go wrong is
in believing that this image produced by "des
Lebens Fremde" is at all appropriate to Wallenstein. They make the mistake of accepting the
construction which Wallenstein puts on his relations with the world, as though it were an objective statement of the truth.

We must not overlook the defensive character of Wallenstein's attitude to the world in the
monologue. The world with its incalculable network of events; the world which challenges Wallenstein's treasonable activity with its adverse
moral judgement – this world is superior to Wallenstein, not inferior. In the concept of "des
Lebens Fremde" we see particularly clearly how
closely the two strands of thought in the monologue coalesce, because the people's rejection,
on moral grounds, of Wallenstein's action, is
one of the factors which are beyond his control.

Wallenstein is no idealist. Far from shrink-
ing back from a materialistic world for fear of
contamination, it is he who is proposing to
contaminate it with his own ruthless ambition.
Far from despising the "alien field of life", he
fears it, because he knows that it is there that
the immoral character of his deed will be exposed. As long as his "deed" has not yet been

accomplished, but is still within his inner self,
it is experienced as an expression of his ambition, his love of power, and the experience is
subjectively pleasurable, because in private he
is able to discount the immoral character of his
aims. But when he sees the deed "out there", exposed to the world's gaze, he sees it through
other people's eyes, and sees it condemned as an
act of treachery. Insisting as he does on the
innocence of the deed so long as it is in the
"secure corner of his heart", he can explain the
appearance of guilt only by referring to "des
Lebens Fremde". But in truth it is not the alien
field of life, not the arena in which the deed
is performed, that is to blame for the guilt
that attaches to Wallenstein: it is the deed itself and the corner of the heart where it orig-
inates, that is the source of his guilt. If the
deed were itself innocent, his conviction of his
moral rectitude would enable him to rebut the
world's false judgement. His attempt in the second section to pass his guilt over as a mere appearance of guilt, is contradicted by other passages (already quoted) in which he admits his
guilt.

In the fourth section of the monologue (192-
218) Wallenstein sees quite clearly that his ambition, if it is to be fulfilled, requires him
to overthrow the power that is rooted in the
childlike faith of the people.

Du willst die Macht,
Die ruhig, sicher thronende erschüttern,
Die in verjährt geheiligtem Besitz,
In der Gewohnheit festgegründet ruht,
Die an der Völker frommem Kinderglauben
Mit tausend zähen Wurzeln sich befestigt.
"You aim to subvert a power which reigns peace-
fully, securely; its age-old sanctified rights
of possession firmly established in custom; a
power which with its innumerable tenacious roots
is based on the people's pious childlike faith."

Wallenstein becomes aware that he is opposed
by a world whose moral assumptions are chall-
enged by his action, so that the moral factor
becomes a threat to his designs exceeding that
of any power or group of powers. This is the
enemy which he really fears, an invisible enemy,
as he calls it, the natural piety in the hearts
of the people.

Ein unsichtbarer Feind ists, den ich fürchte,
Der in der Menschen Brust mir widersteht,
Durch feige Furcht allein mir fürchterlich –

So far it has been made quite clear that the
"invisible enemy" refers to the "people's pious
childlike faith". But Wallenstein refuses to accept the judgement passed on him by the people;
he seeks to belittle it by representing the people as motivated, not by piety and faith, but by
a dull materialistic acceptance of the existing
order of things. This is "das ganz Gemeine", the
"wholly common" or materialistic aspect of life
to which he refers.

Das ganz
Gemeine ists, das ewig Gestrige,
Was immer war und immer wiederkehrt,
Und morgen gilt, weils heute hat gegolten!
Denn aus Gemeinem ist der Mensch gemacht,
Und die Gewohnheit nennt er seine Amma.

But the piety of the people, to which Wallenstein at first refers, does in fact represent
a form of idealism; and it is ironic that Wallenstein, who has largely forfeited his own idealism,should use the phrase,"das ganz Gemeine",
to describe the simple fidelity which is the
common currency of idealism among the people.

The whole monologue represents Wallenstein's
refusal to come to terms with the fact that in
the eyes of the world he is guilty. In the second section he denies the reality of his guilt
and passes it off as a mere appearance produced
by the "ambiguity of life"; in the third section
he projects his guilt on the "alien field of

life", implying that it does not belong to himself, the "doer of the deed", but to the world's judgement; finally in the fourth section he attempts to discredit the moral judgement of the world, describing it in terms of "das ganz Gemeine".

It is an obvious criticism of social and political life to say that it is based too much on habit and custom, and that institutions acquire a certain sanctity simply by virtue of their age; but this does not justify the attempt made by existentialist commentators to use Wallenstein's description to discredit the social and political system presided over by the Austrian Emperor. Wallenstein's reference to "das ganz Gemeine" represents the false construction which he puts on the people's commitment to the moral values handed down to them from the past.

If Wallenstein fears the people, it is not on account of the admixture of materialism, the wholly "common" element, which has partly overlaid their inner faith, that he does so. His true enemy is not "das ganz Gemeine", but the moral faith with which the people's materialism is leavened, faith which is strong enough to enable them to defend their moral order against the traitor.

The reference to the "invisible enemy" which Wallenstein discovers in the hearts of the people, recalls the "heart" or conscience which according to Octavio many a soldier, no matter how devoted he might be to Wallenstein,will discover within himself when the nature of the crime contemplated by Wallenstein is made clear (P.333-6).
Und mancher, der in blindem Eifer jetzt
Zu jedem Äußersten entschlossen scheint,
Findet unerwartet in der Brust ein Herz,
Spricht man des Frevels wahren Namen aus.
The problem dealt with in the fourth section of the monologue is referred to in Schiller's History of this period as follows.

"It was no easy task...to shake to its foundations a legitimate sovereignty, strengthened by time and consecrated by laws and religion.... and to attempt forcibly to uproot those invincible feelings of duty, which plead so loudly and so powerfully in the breast of the subject, in favour of his sovereign" (A.J.W.M.279). The fact that "the poet lets Wallenstein speak as though these moral qualities were only chimeras and out-of-date ideas" (C.H.228), certainly does not justify the inference that Schiller expresses his own view through Wallenstein. As we have said, Wallenstein's reference to "das ganz Gemeine" represents only his own personal attempt to discredit the moral integrity of the people, and so to weaken the effect of their criticism.

It is not only in the monologue that Wallenstein recognises the moral resistance of the people as a serious obstacle to his plans; his fear of such resistance reappears in W.T.1.6. But this time, full of misgivings, he sees the matter more from the point of view of the people. Whatever differences have existed in society, he says, all parties combine together to oppose the "common enemy of mankind", to hunt down the "wild beast" that breaks into the homeland where men have a right to live in security.

Was noch so wütend ringt, sich zu zerstören,
Verträgt,vergleicht sich,den gemeinen Feind
Der Menschlichkeit,das wilde Tier zu jagen,
Das mordend einbricht in die sichre Hürde,
Worin der Mensch geborgen wohnt.(WT.429ff.)

It is a description which highlights the violence of the attack on society, rather than attempting to justify the attack by dwelling on the shortcomings of the society subjected to the attack. "Gemein" here is used primarily in reference to the person who is an enemy to all mankind "in common", but with the recently used phrase "das ganz Gemeine" still echoing in our ears, we can scarcely fail to detect a secondary

sense, which corresponds to the meaning which
the word has in the monologue, except that in
that monologue it is society which is condemned
(by Wallenstein) as "gemein": now it is Wallenstein himself, the "wild beast",who is "gemein".
In this scene Wallenstein virtually confirms
Octavio's reference to the "heart" or the conscience which he says many a soldier under Wallenstein's command will unexpectedly discover in
himself, when his commander's crime is revealed
(P.333-6). Fidelity, says Wallenstein, is every
man's closest blood-brother, whom he feels born
to avenge.

Die Treue, sag ich euch,
Ist jedem Menschen wie der nächste Blutsfreund,
Als ihren Rächer fühlt er sich geboren.WT.424.

The claim made by existentialist critics
that the monologue reveals Wallenstein to be a
revolutionary idealist with a vision of a new
life, is not borne out by the text. It is also
refuted in the very next scene,where he is shown
to be a man without principles, who moreover
considers that he is best served by an army similarly without principles. When in W.T.1.5. the
Swedish colonel Wrangel expresses his fear that
it might not be possible for Wallenstein to win
his army over from their allegiance to the Emperor, Wallenstein replies by pointing out that
whereas the Swedes fight for a cause and follow
their flag with their heart,there is no question
of such commitment in the case of his army.

Ihr Lutherischen fechtet
Für eure Bibel, euch ists um die Sach;
Mit eurem Herzen folgt ihr eurer Fahne...
Von all dem ist die Rede nicht bei uns.WT.297.

When Wrangel exclaims in horror: "Lord God in
heaven! Have people in these parts no homeland,
no hearth and church?" -

Herr Gott im Himmel! Hat man hier zu Lande
Denn keine Heimat,keinen Herd und Kirche?

- Wallenstein seeks to reassure him by referring

to the foreign element in his army, an element
not emotionally attached to any cause. Although
Wrangel is anxious to be reassured that the army
will agree to fight alongside the Swedes, he is
dismayed by the spectacle of an army and an army
commander without principle or faith. There is
a certain irony in Wallenstein's attempt to commend his army to Wrangel as the "scum of the
earth", men who can be relied upon to betray the
Emperor. But he is wrong: he himself is to be
trusted to betray the Emperor, but for the most
his soldiers are not.

Again, in W.T.1.7., where Gräfin Terzky at
last prevails on Wallenstein to make up his
mind, in all the thoughts exchanged between them
there is not one that is concerned with a matter
of principle, or with idealism. It is made clear
that Wallenstein thinks only of his personal interest, of power and ambition. When the Gräfin,
in her description of what it would be like if
he were to go into retirement, stresses the hol-
lowness of any pretensions that he might still
seek to keep up to the position of a great king,
Wallenstein in his reply reveals that the main-
spring of all his actions is his need to maintain his power.

Wenn ich nicht wirke mehr, bin ich vernichtet...
Doch eh ich sinke in die Nichtigkeit,
So klein aufhöre, der so groß begonnen,
Eh mich die Welt mit jenen Elenden
Verwechselt, die der Tag erschafft und stürzt,
Eh spreche Welt und Nachwelt meinen Namen
Mit Abscheu aus, und Friedland sei die Losung
Für jede fluchenswerte Tat.(WT.528-537)

Wallenstein implies that if he could not find
fulfilment by the acquisition of power, he would
in effect be "destroyed", that is as the person
he feels himself to be, as a man of power.Rather
than sink into obscurity, he would prefer that
the world should pronounce his name with loath-
ing, and that Friedland should become a byword

for the most execrable deed. It is not his fall
from power at Regensburg, not the capture of
Sesina, not external "necessity" in any form,
that dictates his act of treason, but the inner
necessity of his own imperious nature.
Compared with this inner motivation of Wallenstein by his overwhelming desire for power,
the need to defend himself against the steps
taken against him by the Emperor, is of little
significance. The answer to Max's argument that
Octavio,by suspecting Wallenstein and in a sense
"wanting him to be guilty", might actually make
him guilty -

> Ja, ihr könntet ihn,
> Weil ihr ihn schuldig wollt,noch schuldig
> machen. (P.2634f.)

- is that Wallenstein is already guilty, and
that it is his guilt which makes it necessary
for Octavio to guard the Emperor against his
treachery. Sometimes the steps taken against
Wallenstein by the Emperor are useful in provid-
ing him with an excuse for his own intrigues;for
as the Gräfin herself points out -

> Was ist so kühn, das Notwehr nicht
> entschuldigt? (WT.548)

Wallenstein in W.T.1.7. reaches his decision to proceed with his rebellion against the
Emperor by means of an act of self-affirmation,
or more accurately affirmation of his desire for
power. This affirmation is expressed in a number
of ways. The Gräfin describes Wallenstein as a
"giant spirit who obeys only himself" (WT.589).
Wallenstein himself admits that he has never
sought to conceal his "boldly aggressive disposition".

> Denn nie hielt ichs der Mühe wert, die kühn
> Umgreifende Gemütsart zu verbergen. (WT.594f.)

Again, the Gräfin speaks of Wallenstein as "remaining true to himself", and elevates his self-
affirmation almost to the level of a moral principle, by declaring that every character who

"agrees with himself" is "right", since there is
no wrong other than inconsistency (WT.597ff.).By
this argument any villain who persists in his
villainy must be considered "right".But sophistry is Gräfin Terzky's speciality. Here is another example.

Die haben Unrecht, die dich fürchteten,
Und doch die Macht dir in die Hände gaben.
                    (WT.598f.)

The Emperor, aware of Wallenstein's lawlessness,
should not have given him command of the army,
even though in doing so he aimed to preserve the
Empire and hoped that Wallenstein's lawlessness
could be controlled. Gräfin Terzky has nothing
to say about the dilemma in which the Emperor
found himself, the need to preserve the Empire
when the only officer capable of doing so was
morally untrustworthy. But Wallenstein himself
is not to be outdone in sophistry. Here is his
contribution.

Es übte der Kaiser
Durch meinen Arm im Reiche Taten aus,
Die nach der Ordnung nie geschehen sollten.
                    (WT.619ff.)

So the Emperor is to be blamed for the lawless
deeds committed by Wallenstein,while he is given
no credit for saving the Empire by employing
Wallenstein. Thus Wallenstein, egged on by the
Gräfin, is urged to accept this conclusion.

Gestehe denn, daß zwischen dir und ihm,
Die Rede nicht kann sein von Pflicht und Recht,
Nur von der Macht und der Gelegenheit!(WT.624)

So Gräfin Terzky contrives to eliminate from the
relation between Wallenstein and the Emperor any
moral element, any question of "duty" or "right",
and to reduce that relation to a mere power-
struggle, in which only "force" and "opportunity" play a part.

Certain critics have regarded Wallenstein's
self-affirmation, whether it is described as
"remaining true to himself" or "agreeing with

himself", as deserving of serious consideration.
We are told that Wallenstein is "not determined
in a merely passive way, but decides...responsi-
bly in favour of his determination by the desire
for power, just as he declines to be determined
by other, moral motives. So he determines himself out of himself...chooses himself...that is,
what he is in his profoundest being...This freedom converts his power-impulse into a will to
power" (W.W.1961.55).

But how are we to envisage this act by which
Wallenstein is said to "choose himself"? If the
self were all of a piece, if it were simple in
character, it is difficult to see in what sense
it could be described as choosing itself; it
would simply exist, with no more power to choose
itself than a stone has. If it is not simple,
then we must ask what faculty fulfils the func-
tion of choosing the self. It must be a faculty
which is able to discriminate between different
functions of the self and to judge them according to some principle.

One could scarcely conceive the task of
choosing the self to be performed by one of the
lower faculties, for instance by the "desire for
power" that is present in Wallenstein. It must
be one of the higher faculties by which the self
is determined. Let us assume that it is Wallenstein's rational or moral faculty which enables
him to choose himself. What sort of self would
he be likely to choose? A higher faculty can
hardly be expected to choose in favour of a desire for power which is nothing more than a
primitive impulse; nor is it likely to elevate
such an impulse to the status of a "will to
power". Therefore one answer to the thesis that
Wallenstein chooses himself by deciding to cultivate his power-impulse, by deliberately converting it into a will to power, and by making
that will to power his sole or his outstanding
motive, is to point out:

(a) that the act of choosing must be carried out by one of the higher faculties, and
(b) that a higher faculty would never decide to make the "will to power" per se the sole or the dominant motive of the self.

Gräfin Terzky praises Wallenstein for being "true to himself", but to what kind of self is he true?He himself has just spoken of his "boldly aggressive disposition", and the Gräfin describes him as the same man that he was eight years earlier, when he passed through Germany with fire and sword. It can scarcely be the moral self to which she refers.

If the act of choosing is carried out by one of the lower faculties,then it is not really carried out at all, and the "will to power" is just another name for the power-impulse. If according to existentialist dogma the choice exercised by the self may well be immoral, this is a dogma that must be rejected, not only because it puts a premium on immoralism, but also on the ground that it is illogical and absurd. A choice in favour of what is immoral, is not a choice at all; it is simply immoralism. This is a point which could scarcely be put more cogently than in the following passage. "God Himself cannot choose what is not good; the freedom of the Almighty hinders not His being determined by what is best...If to break loose from the conduct of reason, and to want that restraint of examination and judgment which keeps us from choosing or doing the worse, be liberty, true liberty, madmen and fools are the only freemen: but yet, I think, nobody would choose to be mad for the sake of such liberty,but he that is mad already" (J.L.347).

Let us look again at the passage which we have been attempting to understand(W.W.1961.55). "He decides...responsibly in favour of his determination by the desire for power, just as he declines to be determined by other,moral motives."

What or who is this "he", this self which is
distinct both from the desire for power and from
moral motives, and is capable of deciding between them? If it cannot be explained to us what
this mysterious neutral faculty is, which chooses between the desire for power and a moral motive, how does it operate or by what criterion
does it choose? "He chooses what he is in his
profoundest being." But is this not just another
way of saying that this faculty simply chooses
the strongest, the most powerful motive? Even if
this mysterious faculty did not exist, would not
the strongest motive prevail in any case? Therefore if this "choosing faculty" exists, it is
simply a measuring device; if it does not exist,
the various motives will record their relative
strengths without its assistance,and the strongest will prevail.

Now let us consider another account of the
way in which the will to power is said to develop in Wallenstein. "We must start with the fact
that it is not at all a question of a decision
involving a choice, but of a decision to carry
out an action which comes upon the acting person
of necessity. So much will-power is deposited in
his self that he cannot but will the deed.A possibility dawns in the world of thought, is taken
over by the will, enters the field of action and
unexpectedly becomes a reality which permits of
no withdrawal. The "pure deed", the growth of an
historical possibility, is transformed and inevitably encloses the doer in itself. Wallenstein
suffers this transformation by the deed, which
brands him a traitor, and his greatness consists in the fact that he is able to take over
this way of being determined, of being a traitor
and nothing else, and yet remaining an acting
person according to his will" (H.R.331). As an
account of Wallenstein's pursuit of power this
scarcely meets the case. He seeks power for its
own sake,or the satisfaction which it gives him;

not for the sake of some noble ideal which it
would enable him to realise. Indeed the passage
which we have been examining (WT.528-537) serves
very well to demonstrate his egocentricity and
lack of idealism.wallenstein does not say:"Rather than forfeit the power which would enable me
to put into practice my all-important ideals, I
am prepared to endure the most appalling reputation as a traitor". What in effect he says is
this: "Rather than sink into obscurity, rather
than be a nobody, I am prepared to endure that
terrible reputation". How is this transformed by
the critic! He first dissociates the desire for
power from its discreditable subjective implica-
tions (greed, self-assertion, vindictiveness),
and then elevates it to a transcendental principle, making it a "possibility in the world of
thought" and an "historical possibility",finally
attributing greatness to Wallenstein for "taking
over" what is in reality nothing more than his
own personal desire for power.

The impulse which makes Wallenstein decide
to affirm his false self, his longing for power,
causes him to use other people, particularly
Thekla, his daughter, as a means to an end. In
W.T.3.4. he speaks of Thekla as a jewel which he
has saved up against the time when she shall
marry into one of the royal families of Europe
(W.T.1531), and he dismisses love as something
which only a soft-hearted middle-class father
would take seriously (W.T.1526-8).

The love of Thekla and Max is the epitome
of pure idealism and stands out in sharp relief
against Wallenstein's materialism. Indeed Thekla
speaks of their love as a sacred treasure rescued so to speak from an imperfect world, to be
preserved only in the innermost depths of their
heart.

Drum laß es uns wie einen heilgen Raub
In unsers Herzens Innerstem bewahren.P.1732f.
Strength in abundance is given to Thekla, and a

"firm will" to fight for the loftiest idealism.

    Ich fühle
Die Kraft mit meinem Glücke mir verliehn...
Den festen Willen hab ich kennenlernen,
Den unbezwinglichen, in meiner Brust,
Und an das Höchste kann ich alles setzen.
                                   (P.1847-53)

Even though Wallenstein has decided to be true
to his false self, it is unlikely that Thekla
will be persuaded to be false to her true self.
Yet in P.3.8. Gräfin Terzky tries to convince
her that there is such a thing as Fate which
will prevent her from "belonging to herself".
She gives Thekla to understand that this is the
kind of Fate that is imposed on all women.

Das Weib soll sich nicht selber angehören,
An fremdes Schicksal ist sie fest gebunden...
                                   (P.1824f.)

But Thekla has another concept of Fate, distinct
from that of imposed Fate; it is indicated in
the following exchanges.

Thekla.So wurde mir im Kloster vorgesagt...
    Ich sei bestimmt,mich leidend ihm zu
                                   opfern.
Gräfin.Das ist dein Schicksal.Füge dich ihm
                                   willig.
    Ich und die Mutter geben dir das
                                   Beispiel.
Thekla.Das Schicksal hat mir den gezeigt,dem ich
    Mich opfern soll,ich will ihm freudig
                                   folgen.
Gräfin.Dein Herz,mein liebes Kind,und nicht das
                                   Schicksal.
Thekla.Der Zug des Herzens ist des Schicksals
                          Stimme.(P.1829ff.)

The idea of "sacrifice", implicit in that of imposed Fate, is contained in Thekla's line, "Ich
sei bestimmt, mich leidend ihm zu opfern", the
"ihm" referring to her father Wallenstein. It is
in lines 1837-8 that Thekla introduces her own
idea of Fate, when she says that Fate has shown

her the one to whom she feels that she should
sacrifice herself, referring of course to Max.At
this point the Gräfin uncharacteristically plays
into her hands, by pointing out that it is not
Fate that has singled out Max for her to sacrifice herself to, but her own heart.

Dein Herz, mein liebes Kind, und nicht das
                    Schicksal. (P.1839)

This gives Thekla the opportunity,in her rejoinder, to stress the importance of her own inner
feelings, her love, by describing the impulse of
the heart as the "voice of Fate".

Der Zug des Herzens ist des Schicksals Stimme.
                                    (P.1840)

The difference between sacrificing herself to
Wallenstein "in suffering" ("leidend", 1834),and
sacrificing herself to Max "joyfully" ("freudig"
1838),is the difference between accepting a destiny that is imposed on her, and on the other
hand spontaneously welcoming a Fate in response
to the impulse of her own heart. We have seen
that in the Gräfin's view a woman, bound as she
is to an "alien Fate", is not to be thought of
as "belonging to herself".

Das Weib soll sich nicht selber angehören.P.1824

But as soon as Thekla has become convinced that
the impulse of her heart is her true destiny,she
declares, in defiance of the Gräfin's pronouncement, that she does in fact belong to herself.

Daß ich mir selbst gehöre, weiß ich nun.(P.1850)

The self which Wallenstein affirms is the self
which seeks above all power:the self which Thekla affirms is her loving self, which is also her
moral self.

There is an unmistakable contrast between
W.T.1.7., in which Wallenstein has revealed the
brutal truth about his desire for power, and on
the other hand W.T.2.2., where in an earnest
conversation with Max the idealist, he has to
keep up a pretence of being an unwilling rebel
compelled by outer "necessity". He adopts the

virtuous pose of a person who is nobly resigned
to doing what is "necessary" or unavoidable,with
a fitting air of dignity.
     So laß uns das Notwendige mit Würde,
     Mit festem Schritte tun...(W.T.834f.)
Has he forgotten that it was no more than two
short scenes ago that he declared his determination to carry out the most execrable deed,rather
than sink into obscurity (WT.535-7)? Such a deed
is "necessary" only in the sense that it answers
to a need within him to satisfy his crude lust
for power.Whether it can be performed with "dignity" seems doubtful.
     When Max denounces the crime of treason,
pleading that it is "as black as hell", Wallenstein deplores such an indelicate statement of
the truth.
     Gleich heißt ihr alles schändlich oder würdig,
  ▸ Bös oder gut...   (W.T.783f.)
Rather than have his action condemned as evil,
he prefers to suppress the distinction between
good and evil, hiding behind ambiguity, which is
also present in his statement that one can remain "pure" only if one goes through life without having any "desire" or "purpose".
     –Ja, wer durchs Leben gehet ohne Wunsch,
     Sich jeden Zweck versagen kann, der wohnt
     Im leichten Feuer mit dem Salamander,
     Und hält sich rein im reinen Element.WT.793ff.
He does not say what sort of "desire" or "purpose" he is referring to. The possibility of remaining "pure" depends upon going through life,
not without any desire or purpose at all, but
without a wicked desire or a purpose that is
dishonourable.
     We must compare Wallenstein's reply to Max's
criticism, with the more convincing reply given
by Octavio in P.5.1., where Max criticises him
for spying on Wallenstein.
     Mein bester Sohn! Es ist nicht immer möglich,
     Im Leben sich so kinderrein zu halten,

Wie's uns die Stimme lehrt im Innersten.
In steter Notwehr gegen arge List
Bleibt auch das redliche Gemüt nicht wahr –
Das eben ist der Fluch der bösen Tat,
Daß sie, fortzeugend,immer Böses muß gebären.
Ich klügle nicht, ich tue meine Pflicht,
Der Kaiser schreibt mir mein Betragen vor.
Wohl wär es besser, überall dem Herzen
Zu folgen, doch darüber würde man
Sich manchen guten Zweck versagen müssen.
Hier gilts, mein Sohn,dem Kaiser wohl zu dienen,
Das Herz mag dazu sprechen, was es will.P.2447ff

In the first place, whereas Wallenstein
is silent about the nature of his "desire" or
"purpose", Octavio more than once refers to the
idealism which should inspire a man in his jour-
ney through life. "The voice within"("die Stimme
im Innersten"), the "honest soul" ("das redliche
Gemüt"), and "following one's heart" – these are
the expressions with which Octavio refers to his
inner moral self. If circumstances do not always
permit him, he says, to "follow his heart", that
is to act directly on his moral impulse, nevertheless in pursuing "many a good purpose" (2458)
which critics might consider morally dubious, he
always has in mind the general good purpose of
upholding the moral order represented by the
Emperor himself.

Octavio's justification for the regrettable
means which he has to employ, is the necessity
of carrying out, on behalf of the Emperor, a defensive action against Wallenstein's treasonable
plans ("Notwehr gegen arge List"). If, in Octavio's words, "it is not always possible in life
to retain the purity of a child" (2447f.), this
means that despite one's good intentions, one
sometimes has to adopt the world's way of deal-
ing with the world's evil. By way of contrast,
Wallenstein, far from having any good intentions
which would justify his actions, is himself responsible for the "curse of the evil deed" to

which Octavio refers, the evil deed which engen-
ders evil (2452f.). When Octavio refers to the
Emperor as prescribing what he must do (2455),
and adds that he must serve the Emperor, whatever his "heart" or conscience feels about it
(2459f.), he is simply pointing out that the
Emperor,as a practical politician and statesman,
must sometimes adopt the world's method of deal-
ing for instance with treason, must employ materialistic measures on behalf of the moral order
which he is defending. There is, it is true, a
certain tension between Octavio's idealism, the
action which his heart urges him to take, and on
the other hand the practical policy laid down by
the Emperor; but if Octavio agrees to carry out
that policy, he does so, not in a spirit of servile submission, but because he himself sees the
need for it. Finally, it is only the means that
have to be adopted which Octavio's "heart" or
conscience, his ideal self, sometimes regrets.
The purpose, the upholding of the moral order,
is one to which he gives his full consent.

The misconceptions that abound concerning
the relations between Octavio and Wallenstein,
and between both of them and the Emperor, are
brought out in remarks made by commentators on
this speech. To maintain that Octavio loses his
integrity by betraying his friend, is to misrep-
resent the situation by omitting the main factor
involved. It is self-evident that duty to one's
country, particularly in wartime, takes prece-
dence over personal friendship. To assert that
the Emperor is discredited because he is served
by a man who betrays his friend, is to stand the
truth on its head. Had Octavio in the name of
friendship connived at Wallenstein's perfidy, he
would have compounded Wallenstein's crime by his
own treachery. In that case the Emperor would
indeed have been discredited. Nothing could be
more absurd than the suggestion that Wallenstein
is to be pardoned for betraying the Emperor on

the ground put forward by Wallenstein himself, that the Emperor is not his friend (WT.2119ff.). None but personal friends of the Emperor owe their country any loyalty - that would seem to be the logical inference.

Octavio's good motives are evident enough in the play itself, and it should not have been necessary for Schiller to spring to his defence in his letter to K.Böttiger dated 1 March 1799.

"To be sure (Octavio) chooses a bad means, but he pursues a good purpose. He wants to save the State and serve the Emperor, whom after God he regards as the highest authority to whom all duty is owed. He betrays a friend who trusts him,but this friend is a traitor to his Emperor."

The point that Schiller makes in stating that the service which Octavio renders to the Emperor is subject to his duty to God, is confirmed by a passage in P.5.1. When Max asks Octavio how he proposes to disarm Wallenstein in the midst of his army, surrounded by his thousands, he refers to Wallenstein as the "Mighty One".

Dieses Blatt hier - dieses! willst du geltend
                              machen?
Den Mächtigen in seines Heeres Mitte,
Umringt von seinen Tausenden, entwaffnen?P.2509.

Octavio's reply is that he is in the hands of the "Almighty".

Ich stehe in der Allmacht Hand; sie wird
Das fromme Kaiserhaus mit ihrem Schilde
Bedecken,und das Werk der Nacht zertrümmern.
                              (P.2514-6)

The moral order which Octavio has previously mentioned as the principle for which he works, is now associated with God, and it is because the imperial cause is "pious" that it enjoys the protection of God. There is nothing ambiguous about Octavio's references to the two opposed causes. Wallenstein's cause is described as the "work of night" ("das Werk der Nacht",P.2516),

and the imperial cause, to which Octavio is convinced many of Wallenstein's men will defect, is
the "good cause".

...auch im Lager
Gibt es der braven Männer gnug, die sich
Zur guten Sache munter schlagen werden.P.2517-9.

An important consequence of Wallenstein's
decision to renounce his loyalty to the Emperor,
is that Max now has to choose between his own
allegiance to the Emperor and on the other hand
the idealistic friendship which binds him to
Wallenstein. As the latter points out, although
up to now Max has had no difficulty in making
the right moral decisions, this will scarcely be
so in future.

Sanft wiegte dich bis heute dein Geschick,
Du konntest spielend deine Pflichten üben,
Jedwedem schönen Trieb Genüge tun,
Mit ungeteiltem Herzen immer handeln.
So kanns nicht ferner bleiben.WT.719ff.

Wallenstein is confident that Max, obliged to
choose between morality and friendship, and subjected to his friend's powerful influence, will
not be able to avoid betraying his moral principles. In Wallenstein's description Max has so
far performed his duties "playfully" or effort-
lessly, he has given expression to every "beautiful impulse", and has always acted with an "un-
divided heart". In short Wallenstein so to speak
unwittingly describes Max as a "beautiful soul",
without really understanding what is implied by
his description, namely that Max is a person
whose moral principles are rooted in his very
nature. It follows that Max, despite his friendship with Wallenstein, will not be easily persuaded (as Wallenstein supposes) to support him
in his betrayal of the Emperor.

By the time that Max and his father meet in
a farewell scene in W.T.2.7. the pressure of events makes a decision by Max the more urgent:
Wallenstein has dispatched his messengers to

Prag and Eger, and Octavio for his part has pre-
vailed over Isolani and Buttler to defect from
Wallenstein. Max soon shows that his confidence
in his moral instinct is undiminished by the
difficult choice which he will have to make. On
three occasions in this scene he refers to his
"heart", that is his conscience or moral instinct as the principle by which alone he will
make his decision, in defiance of whatever pressure may be put upon him,from whatever source.
When Octavio exclaims - "Max! In the Emperor's
name, follow me!" - he receives this reply.
Kein Kaiser hat dem Herzen vorzuschreiben.1230.
Max means that if he decides to remain loyal to
the Emperor, the decision will not be dictated
to him by the Emperor or his representative Oct-
avio:it will be the decision of his own "heart",
his own free moral decision. Secondly when Octavio, distressed to think that Max, unable to
tear himself away from Thekla, might for that
reason decide to stay with Wallenstein, exclaims
- "Oh,come, my son, and save your virtue!" - Max
again replies that he will be guided solely by
his "heart" or conscience.
Dem Herzen folg ich, denn ich darf ihm trauen.
                                    (WT.1247)
It is perhaps implied in this passage that Max
is confident of his ability to resolve any conflict that might arise between his "heart" in
the sense of his love of Thekla, and his "heart"
in the sense of his conscience; because his love
and his moral sense are so closely associated.
     Thirdly when Octavio questions whether Max
will always have the power to follow his heart,
Max replies that Wallenstein will be no more
successful than Octavio has been in forcing his
heart to make its decision by any means other
than that of its own natural morality.
Du hast des Herzens Stimme nicht bezwungen,
So wenig wird der Herzog es vermögen.(WT.1262ff)
     Just as Max must resist any pressure put

upon him either by Octavio or Wallenstein, so
Thekla must withstand the attempt of the domin-
eering Gräfin Terzky to coerce her. It matters
nothing at all to the latter that the love between Thekla and Max is a form of idealism, that
it is, as Max says, the only pure and undefiled
thing in a world of deceit and hypocrisy, murder
and poison, perjury and treason.
Betrug ist überall und Heuchelschein,
Und Mord und Gift und Meineid und Verrat,
Der einzig reine Ort ist unsre Liebe,
Der unentweihte in der Menschlichkeit.WT.1218.
In W.T.3.2. the Gräfin tells Thekla bluntly that
Wallenstein proposes to desert the Emperor and
join forces with the enemy, and that at this
critical juncture Thekla must play a key part by
making use of Max's love to bind him to her
father (W.T.1309f.). Octavio refers to this intrigue as a "net" thrown over Max ("Ich sehe das
Netz geworfen über ihn", P.595), and he repeats
this metaphor in a warning to Max (P.2311,2379).
Thekla herself is clear-sighted in detecting the
intrigue; she warns Max of the Gräfin's ulterior
motive (P.1685f.). In using Max's love for her
own purpose, Gräfin Terzky shows scarcely any
respect for him as a morally responsible person.
When she regrets that he appears to be loyal to
the Emperor, Thekla comments: "No more than duty
and honour require of him". The Gräfin replies:
Von seiner Liebe fordert man Beweise,
Und nicht von seiner Ehre - Pflicht und Ehre!
Das sind vieldeutig doppelsinnge Namen,
Ihr sollt sie ihm auslegen, seine Liebe
Soll seine Ehre ihm erklären. (W.T.1315ff.)
"We want proof of his love, not of his honour -
duty and honour! Those are equivocal, ambiguous
names. You must interpret them for him; his love
must explain to him what honour is."
    We have seen that Wallenstein's appeal to
the "ambiguity of life" is a device which he em-
ploys in an attempt to conceal his guilt. In the

present case the Gräfin's dismissal of moral
qualities as ambiguous so obviously serves her
private purpose, that it is surprising that the
idea of ambiguity should ever have been accepted
as founded on an objective truth of the play.The
Gräfin's purpose is that Thekla should persuade
Max to remain loyal to her father, and that he
should therefore become disloyal to the Emperor;
it follows that if Max regards duty and honour
as requiring him to remain loyal to the Emperor,
this will be an impediment to the fulfilment of
the Gräfin's purpose. Therefore the Gräfin urges
Thekla to persuade Max that duty and honour require him to be loyal, not to the Emperor, but
to Wallenstein. Thekla could of course attempt
to do so by rational argument, but that is not
the suggestion: love is to play a part, in fact
"love must explain his honour to him". In order
to make her meaning absolutely clear, the Gräfin
adds: "He is to renounce either the Emperor or
you" ("Er soll dem Kaiser oder Euch entsagen",
W.T.1320). Is it not beyond doubt that what this
cynical woman means is that disloyalty to the
Emperor is the price that Max must pay for Thekla's love, that love is the bribe that is to be
dangled in front of him, to induce him to be
disloyal to the Emperor? It is not with any supposed ambiguity of the concepts of duty and honour that the Gräfin is concerned, but with the
undermining of Max's sense of duty and honour.
Just as in W.T.1.7. she encourages Wallenstein,
in his relations with the Emperor, to replace
moral principles ("duty" and "right") with practical considerations of "force" and "opportunity" (supra 106), so here she hopes that with
Thekla's cooperation she will induce Max to sacrifice his moral principles to his love. It is
Thekla's responsibility to see that Max, by remaining on Wallenstein's side, will set an example which will be followed by the rest of the
army.

Es braucht ein großes Beispiel, die Armee
Ihm nachzuziehn. Die Piccolomini
Stehn bei dem Heer in Ansehn...
Ihr habt jetzt viel in Eurer Hand.WT.1332ff.

By resorting to such a device in an attempt to
secure the continued allegiance of the army,
Gräfin Terzky reveals the degree to which Wallenstein's authority has been weakened by his
disloyalty to the Emperor. In.W.T.3.5-10 he receives a steady stream of news informing him of
the desertion of one general after another, one
regiment after another. The weakness of his position is again revealed by the subterfuge to
which he has recourse when in W.T.3.15. men of
the Pappenheim regiment seek reassurance concerning his loyalty to the Emperor. He poses as
a champion of "peace" and argues that they must
accept what he calls the offer of help made by
the Swedes. Above all he uses something that is
sacred, personal friendship and loyalty, for his
own purpose, appealing to his soldiers' "heart"
("Euer Herz sei meine Festung!",W.T.1916f.), and
making a display of his own "heart", which he
claims beats in sympathy with the German people
in their suffering.

                                    Ich hab
Ein Herz, der Jammer dieses deutschen Volks
                    erbarmt mich. W.T.1976f.
His posturing and pathos is brought to an abrupt
end by Buttler, who announces that the imperial
eagle is being removed from his standards, and
replaced by his own insignia (W.T.1994-6).

    An ironic light is thrown on Wallenstein's
pose as a man of peace, when in W.T.3.18. Max
describes him as following only the wild impulse
of his heart, like some blind, soulless natural
force.
Wie das gemütlos blinde Element,
Das furchtbare,mit dem kein Bund zu schließen,
Folgst du des Herzens wildem Trieb allein.
                    (W.T.2091-3)

Max goes on to describe Wallenstein's actions in
terms of a furiously erupting volcano, pouring
forth a destructive stream of lava, laying waste
the land and wiping out the work of man.

Schnell,unverhofft,bei nächtlich stiller Weile
Gärts in dem tückschen Feuerschlunde, ladet
Sich aus mit tobender Gewalt, und weg
Treibt über alle Pflanzungen der Menschen
Der wilde Strom in grausender Zerstörung.
(W.T.2097ff.)

Max's tragic description of Wallenstein's essen-
tially destructive character, forms a stark contrast to the kind of remark which Max made earlier in the play when he put up a spirited defence of Wallenstein as a man of peace (e.g.P.
569ff.). The critic who accepts such a comment
on Wallenstein, made by Max at a time when he
was still blind to his hero's defects, and who
gives it prominence as though it were the gospel
truth, is strangely reluctant to refer to the
passage just quoted, a passage which reflects
Max's judgement after he has at last discovered
the truth about Wallenstein.

A similar description of Wallenstein's de-
monic existence has been given by his wife the
Duchess (W.T.1380ff.). Indeed Wallenstein himself, in his remarkable speech in W.T.3.18.,re-
fers to himself as a star which goes off course
and projects itself in a fiery ball against a
neighbouring world, setting it alight.

Und wenn der Stern, auf dem du lebst und wohnst,
Aus seinem Gleise tritt, sich brennend wirft
Auf eine nächste Welt und sie entzündet.WT.2186.

It is almost as though Wallenstein regarded
his downfall and the resulting destruction as
itself a demonstration of his power. Those who
are likely to be involved are not without a certain sense of foreboding, to which Max gives expression in P.2639f.

Denn dieser Königliche, wenn er fällt,
Wird eine Welt im Sturze mit sich reißen.

We have seen that in his speech to the Pappenheim regiment Wallenstein tries to appeal to the hearts of his men, the affection and devotion that they have had for him in the past, in an attempt to persuade them to remain loyal to him. In his appeal to Max it is even more evident that he attempts to make use of their mutual affection in order to avoid losing such a popular and influential officer. There is no doubt that the affection between them is genuine enough. He describes how, when Max as a tender boy was weakened by exposure to the cold,he even acted as his nurse, until Max - warmed against his heart - gradually revived (W.T.2152f.).

Bis du von mir erwärmt, an meinem Herzen,
Das junge Leben wieder freudig fühltest.

He speaks of the many men whom he has rewarded with land and honours, and then declares that it is Max alone whom he has loved, Max alone to whom he has given his heart, his very self.

...dich hab ich geliebt,
Mein Herz, mich selber hab ich dir gegeben.

Max, he says, is attached to him by every tender feeling of the soul,by every holy tie of nature.

Du bist an mich
Geknüpft mit jedem zarten Seelenbande,
Mit jeder heilgen Fessel der Natur...

He declares that if Max deserts him, he will demonstrate that the "most sacred feeling" has meant nothing to him.

...Daß dir das heiligste Gefühl nichts galt.

But even as he speaks of the "sacredness" of friendship, he is attempting to use it to influence Max's decision, indeed using it for the same purpose as that for which Gräfin Terzky tries to persuade Thekla to use Max's love - to induce him to give up his allegiance to the Emperor.Wallenstein's persuasive rhetoric in praise of friendship is marred by the use of the image of the notorious "net", that symbol of worldly intrigue which is so conspicuously out of key

with the theme of idealistic friendship. After
referring to the "net of love" that he has spun
round Max, he challenges him to tear himself
free, if he can.

Ein Liebesnetz hab ich um dich gesponnen,
Zerreiß es, wenn du kannst. (W.T.2166f.)

It is a strange friendship in which one of the
friends deprives the other of his freedom. The
references to the power wielded over Max by Wallenstein increase as the latter reaches his per-
oration. From line 2179 the speech becomes more
and more an expression of Wallenstein's determination to dominate Max, to deprive him of his
independent will, and almost to compel him to
renounce his allegiance to the Emperor. "Do you
belong to yourself? Are you your own commander,
do you stand free in the world as I do, so that
you could be the doer of your deeds? It is upon
me that you are planted, I am your Emperor; to
belong to me and obey me - that is your honour
and your natural law."

                          Gehörst
Du dir? Bist du dein eigener Gebieter,
Stehst frei da in der Welt wie ich, daß du
Der Täter deiner Taten könntest sein?
Auf mich bist du gepflanzt, ich bin dein Kaiser,
Mir angehören, mir gehorchen, das
Ist deine Ehre, dein Naturgesetz.

The irony that pervades this passage arises
from the echoes of earlier passages which are
awakened, passages which refute the claims made
by Wallenstein on his own behalf, as well as his
criticism of Max. The first of Wallenstein's
questions, "Gehörst du dir?", reminds us of the
argument advanced by Gräfin Terzky in an attempt
to convince Thekla that she is subject to her
father's will; a woman does not belong to herself, she maintains, because she is bound to a
Fate that is alien to her (supra 111); which
passage in turn reminds us that Wallenstein, although he attempts to control Fate, is himself

controlled by it. We also recall Thekla's belief
that love, the "impulse of the heart", is the
voice of a very different kind of Fate (P.1840),
which assures her that she does in fact "belong
to herself" (P.1850). Max too is possessed of
such an inner principle of love and moral idealism, by virtue of which he too can claim that he
"belongs to himself".

"Bist du dein eigener Gebieter?" is Wallenstein's second question. Is Max his own master,
is he a person who obeys his own "commands" or
"commandments", who acts on his own principles?
The question is answered in the affirmative in
the passage in W.T.2.2., where Max warns Wallenstein that if he committed treason,it would have
the effect of confirming the general scepticism
concerning the ability of man, "freely" or on
his own responsibility to achieve "nobility" or
morality, that is moral freedom.
Recht geben würd es dem gemeinen Wahn,
Der nicht an Edles in der Freiheit glaubt...
                    (W.T.759f.)
When Wallenstein asks Max whether he stands
free in the world, so that he could be the "doer
of his deed", the question recalls the third
section of the monologue, in which Wallenstein
describes his "deed" as "his" so long as it remains within him, in the "secure corner of his
heart", though it is no longer "his" when it enters the "alien field of life" (W.T.186ff.). In
our comment on that passage we pointed out that
if Wallenstein's deed is doomed once it enters
the alien world, this is so because the world's
condemnation of his deed cannot be rebutted by
his own conviction of his moral rectitude. Since
Max does in fact act on the principle of "nobility in freedom" or moral freedom, since he does
indeed act on a moral principle to which he is
committed, he unlike Wallenstein, is truly the
"doer of his deed".
If after claiming that he "stands free in

the world" (W.T.2181), Wallenstein a few lines
later (2186f.) mentions the possibility of going
off course, it is by reference to his neglect of
the moral factor that we must explain that danger, since it is through his "invisible enemy",
that moral sense in the heart of every man,caus-
ing the defection of so many regiments, that it
has become clear that Wallenstein has already
gone off course. In telling Max that he cannot
choose whether he will follow him in his erratic
course –
Du kannst nicht wählen, ob du folgen willst...
– he is really saying that Max must renounce his
moral responsibility as he himself has done, but
by bringing out the tragic consequences of abdi-
cating his moral responsibility and going off
course, Wallenstein has made it less, not more
likely that Max, who as a beautiful soul, has
his moral sense firmly rooted in his nature,
will follow his example.

When Max hesitates in W.T.3.21, and speaks
of the two voices that are contending against
each other within him, and of the night that has
descended upon his soul, so that he has difficulty in choosing the right course (W.T.2279ff),
the choice that he finds so hard to make, is not
a choice between the inner voice of idealism and
the outer voice of the world with its materialistic values, but a choice between two different
forms of idealism: loyalty on the one hand to
the legitimate authority of the Emperor, and on
the other to idealistic love and friendship.
There is no question of his sacrificing his integrity, his idealism, to materialistic values.

As regards his political loyalty, Max vows
faithfully to return to the Emperor the regiments entrusted to him, and if he fails to keep
his vow he is prepared to die (W.T.2243ff.).
Die Regimenter, die mir anvertraut sind,
Dem Kaiser treu hinwegzuführen, hab ich
Gelobt, dies will ich halten oder sterben.

There is no indecision here, no weakening of his
idealism. It is not a sign of weakness that Max
should consult Thekla before making his decision, because she will be affected by it. Relying on her idealism, he knows that her voice
will be the voice of truth, not falsified by any
personal interest, but drawn from the pure foun-
tain of light itself (W.T.2295ff.).

Wo ist eine Stimme
Der Wahrheit, der ich folgen darf? Uns alle
Bewegt der Wunsch, die Leidenschaft. Daß jetzt
Ein Engel mir vom Himmel niederstiege,
Das Rechte mir, das unverfälschte, schöpfte
Am reinen Lichtquell, mit der reinen Hand!

Thekla made up her mind as early as W.T.3.2.When
Gräfin Terzky told her of her father's decision
to betray the Emperor, and appealed to her to
cooperate, in which case all would be well, she
immediately replied both by condemning Wallenstein's action and by rejecting the suggestion
that she and Max should condone that action in
order to gain personal advantage (W.T.1355f.).

When Max, in W.T.3.21, asks Thekla to let
her "heart" decide, she replies: "Yours has long
since decided; follow your first feeling."

O das deine
Hat längst entschieden, folge dem ersten
Gefühl -   (W.T.2337ff.)

So much for the belief that Max cannot make up
his own mind. He refers the matter to Thekla because it must be a joint decision of the idealism which they share,but she cannot add anything
to what he has already decided. She knows that
Max, guided by his "tender heart" or beautiful
soul, has instinctively discovered the right
path which he must follow (W.T.2339ff.).

Wie könnte das
Das Rechte sein, was dieses zarte Herz
Nicht gleich zuerst ergriffen und gefunden?

There is nothing ambiguous about the words with
which she urges Max to "go and fulfil his duty".

Geh und erfülle deine Pflicht. (W.T.2342)
Nor does she let her personal interest cloud her
clear-sighted judgment that her father is guilty
(W.T.2357). Nor is there any equivocation in the
earnestness with which she urges Max to begone.
"Hasten to separate your good cause from our unhappy one!" (W.T.2353).
- Fort! Eile! Eile, deine gute Sache
Von unsrer unglückseligen zu trennen.
Thus it is quite misleading to suggest that Max
learns to sacrifice his integrity and reach a
compromise with the questionable values of the
world. On the contrary what he learns is that he
must strictly separate his "good cause",his idealism, from Wallenstein's "unhappy cause",which
is tainted with ambition and treachery.

Wallenstein is brought down by that aspect
of Fate which we call Nemesis or retribution. It
is useless to pretend that this cannot be true,
on the ground that it suggests that the world of
"Wallenstein" is a place where the righteous and
the unrighteous reap the rewards of their actions,a view which it is maintained is inconsistent with the death of the blameless Max. The
textual evidence of the working of Nemesis in
the case of Wallenstein himself is too strong to
be ignored. Secondly, it is a mistake to assume
that, because one person is punished for the
crime he commits, it follows that all people
reap the rewards of their actions. Why should it
be supposed that Schiller should portray a world
which would bear no resemblance to the world in
which we live, which is a world where some people get what they deserve and others do not?
Thirdly the death of Max may have a very different meaning from the fate which overtakes Wallenstein.

We associate the idea of Nemesis with that
of justice; it is a moral concept.Octavio's pro-
phecy (P.333-6) that when the full extent of
Wallenstein's treachery is made known, many a

soldier will find within him a "heart" or conscience to condemn it, proves to be true; and
the resolve of many of his regiments to desert
him, plays a decisive part in his downfall. We
also recall Wallenstein's own reference to the
"invisible enemy" which he fears in the heart of
every man (W.T.203f.), as well as his description of fidelity as every man's blood-brother,
whom he feels born to avenge (W.T.424-6).

But we have to consider how Schiller de-
picts the force of Nemesis as operating in a
play about Wallenstein during the Thirty Years'
War, at a time when lawlessness is widespread,
and morality is maintained only with difficulty.
A passage in W.T.1.7. spoken by Wallenstein when
he has decided to commit himself to hostilities
against the Emperor, gives us a clearer insight
into the working of Nemesis in this play.

Es ist sein böser Geist und meiner. Ihn
Straft er durch mich,das Werkzeug seiner
                    Herrschsucht,
Und ich erwart es, daß der Rache Stahl
Auch schon für meine Brust geschliffen ist.
                    (W.T.645-8)

Wallenstein describes the "punishment", the "revenge" or retribution that is inflicted on this
or that participant in the power-struggle, as
having its source within the power-struggle itself. The spirit of retribution will punish the
the Emperor through Wallenstein, and it is implied that it will be the Emperor who will serve
as the instrument of retribution in the case of
Wallenstein. The idea of Nemesis which underlies
the play consists so to speak in an unwritten
law that he who seeks to dominate the struggle
for power and to become all-powerful, must run
the risk of being struck down as an act of retribution. From this point of view it is only a
very rough justice that Fate dispenses in the
form of Nemesis, a contingent justice arising
from the determination of the contending forces

to obstruct the attempt of any individual to exercise absolute power.

In the passage quoted (W.T.645-8) Wallenstein discounts the distinction between the legitimate ruler of a country and the military commander who owes him allegiance; and he attributes to the Emperor the "ambition" which belongs
to himself. The Emperor is not just another participant in the power-struggle, as Wallenstein
regards him;he is the defender of a moral order.
Nevertheless in the materialistic world of the
Thirty Years' War, the Emperor, in defending
that order, cannot but resort to materialistic
means. The contribution made to the process of
Nemesis by the power-struggle itself, is but one
example of the way in which moral purposes are
effected by materialistic means.

Just as the Emperor was forced by "bitter
necessity" to employ Wallenstein as the only man
capable of defending the Empire against its enemies (W.T.570f.), so he is forced to dispense
with his services when his treason is no longer
supportable. In each case the means which he has
to employ contradict his moral purpose. In the
first case Wallenstein by his lawlessness betrays the Emperor's idealistic aim of preserving
the Empire; in the second case the Emperor, by
outlawing Wallenstein, shows that he is obliged
to accept the assistance of any person, however
base, however materialistic, thus consigning the
fate of Wallenstein to the crude aspect of Nemesis, working through the power-struggle.

That it is Buttler in W.T.4.1. who speaks
in the name of Fate -
Bis hieher, Friedland, und nicht weiter! sagt
Die Schicksalsgöttin.   (W.T.2433f.)
- and that it is Buttler who declares that Wal-
lenstein may well be destroyed by the power of
Nemesis (W.T.2443f.) -
Nimm dich in acht! dich treibt der böse Geist
Der Rache - daß dich Rache nicht verderbe!

- has generally been regarded by critics as inappropriate. They are of course right, if they
regard Nemesis as a pure principle of justice.
But if we accept that in this play portraying
the lawless times of the Thirty Years' War, Nemesis acts, not as a pure principle of justice,
but as a rough-and-ready principle of retribution, then we may well come to the conclusion
that it is not after all so inappropriate that
Buttler should be the mouthpiece of this cruder
aspect of Nemesis. The retribution that overtakes Wallenstein is decreed by the Emperor acting in the interest of the nation, but it is effected by Buttler acting on a desire for revenge
in a private matter. The conflict between the
Emperor and Wallenstein is of necessity inter-
linked with the whole network of the universal
power-struggle in all its ramifications. The
part played by Buttler in the downfall of Wallenstein, as well as the contributions made by
the two mercenaries Macdonald and Deveroux, who
are prepared to murder anyone provided that they
are paid -
Wir sind Soldaten der Fortuna, wer
Das meiste bietet, hat uns.(WT.3239f.)
- accurately reflect the materialistic aspect of
the power-struggle.
    We have seen that Wallenstein, a slave to
his ambition, never achieves moral freedom; in
fact he tends to reject the very possibility of
achieving it, preferring to believe in a force
of Necessity which rules out moral freedom. Similarly, in a passage which reads almost like a
parody of Wallenstein's tendency to justify his
actions by appealing to "Necessity", Buttler
claims that what he intended to be his own free
action, is really the work of "fearful Necessity" working through him (W.T.2873ff.).
Doch nicht mein Haß macht mich zu seinem
                            Mörder.
Sein böses Schicksal ists...

Es denkt der Mensch die freie Tat zu tun,
Umsonst! Er ist das Spielwerk nur der blinden
Gewalt, die aus der eignen Wahl ihm schnell
Die furchtbare Notwendigkeit erschafft.
We are reminded of the passage in W.T.1.7. where
Wallenstein refers to the power possessed by
Fate over a man's heart, to force him to act in
a certain way (W.T.655f.).
Recht stets behält das Schicksal, denn das Herz
In uns ist sein gebietrischer Vollzieher.

A legend appears to have sprung up among
certain interpreters of this play, that Octavio
is responsible for the assassination of Wallenstein, even though the deed is carried out by
Buttler. Once such a legend has established itself, it tends to be regarded as proven by the
majority of critics, who therefore consider an
examination of the evidence superfluous.Further-
more the legend is welcome to those who are anxious to represent Wallenstein as an existentialist hero,and who are for that reason glad enough
to see his opponent discredited. It is all the
more important, in the interest of the truth,
that the evidence should be examined.

It is maintained that in W.T.2.6. Octavio
gives Buttler permission to assassinate Wallenstein. It is in this scene that Octavio convin-
ces Buttler that he was previously mistaken in
believing that Wallenstein recommended him to
the court in Vienna for the title of Count: in
reality, says Octavio, Wallenstein secretly ad-
vised the court against granting the title. In
this way Octavio estranges Buttler from Wallenstein; but the assertion that Buttler in this
scene obtains Octavio's consent to the assassination of Wallenstein is contradicted by the
evidence of the text.

When Octavio urges Buttler to leave Wallenstein as quickly as possible, the following dia-
logue ensues.
Octavio.Schnell trennt Euch von dem Herzog.1167.

Buttler. Mich von ihm trennen!
Octavio.   Wie? Bedenkt Ihr Euch?
Buttler (furchtbar ausbrechend).
          Nur von ihm trennen? O! er soll nicht
                                        leben!
Octavio.
Folgt mir nach Frauenberg, wo alle Treuen (1170)
Bei Gallas sich und Altringer versammeln.
Viel andre bracht ich noch zu ihrer Pflicht
Zurück, heut Nacht entfliehen sie aus Pilsen.

The two men are really at cross purposes;
for while Buttler is preoccupied with thoughts
of revenge against Wallenstein, Octavio is bent
on making sure that Buttler can be trusted to
commit himself to the Emperor's side by fleeing
from Wallenstein. When Buttler echoes Octavio by
exclaiming "I leave him!", Octavio is worried
lest he should be having second thoughts ("Wie?
Bedenkt Ihr Euch?"). When Buttler "breaks out
fearfully" - "Only leave him? Oh, he shouldn't
be alive!" (1169) - Octavio, far from taking
Buttler's last remark literally, is reassured to
find that Buttler shows no sign of hesitating
about defecting from Wallenstein. He therefore
asks him to follow him to Frauenberg, where the
other defectors are gathering, which is scarcely
the reaction to be expected if he had received
the startling news that Buttler intended to kill
Wallenstein.

Buttler is now in something of a quandary.
On the one hand he does not wish to go to Frauenberg with Octavio, because he plans to stay
with Wallenstein in order to await an opportunity to assassinate him; but on the other hand he
must conceal his intention from Octavio, who as
he knows would not countenance such a barbaric
action against Wallenstein.

Buttler ist heftig auf und ab gegangen,und tritt
zu Octavio mit entschlossenem Blick.
          Graf Piccolomini! Darf Euch der Mann
          Von Ehre sprechen,der die Treue brach?1175

Octavio.Der darf es, der so ernstlich es bereut.
Buttler.So laßt mich hier, auf Ehrenwort.
Octavio.   Was sinnt Ihr?
Buttler.Mit meinem Regimente laßt mich bleiben.
Octavio.Ich darf Euch traun. Doch sagt mir, was
                                    Ihr brütet?
Buttler.Die Tat wirds lehren.Fragt mich jetzt
                        nicht weiter. (1180)
Traut mir! Ihr könnts! Bei Gott! Ihr überlasset
Ihn seinem guten Engel nicht! – Lebt wohl!
                Geht ab

When Buttler appeals to Octavio to let him stay
with Wallenstein "on his word of honour" (1177),
he is giving his word that he will in due course
withdraw his regiment from Wallenstein's command
and return it to the imperial army. We have seen
that this is the point on which Octavio seeks
reassurance, and Buttler is anxious to satisfy
him on this point, since otherwise Octavio might
not agree to his staying with Wallenstein, in
which case he would be prevented from carrying
out the assassination. (Later,when Buttler gives
Gordon the false impression that he has given
his word of honour to assassinate Wallenstein
(W.T.2692ff.), this is obviously an invention on
his part, designed to convince Gordon that he
has committed himself to the deed and that there
is no drawing back from it.)

     Buttler's request renews the doubts in Oct-
avio's mind concerning the genuineness of Buttler's defection from Wallenstein. It is therefore on this point that he seeks reassurance
from Buttler, i.e. in a matter which is quite
distinct from any suspicion that Buttler might
intend harm to Wallenstein. But when he asks him
straight out: "Was sinnt Ihr?" (W.T.1177), "What
are you planning?", Buttler shirks the question,
simply repeating his request to be allowed to
stay (1178). Octavio, having just succeeded in
winning Buttler over from his allegiance to Wallenstein, does not wish to give the impression

that he mistrusts him, but he feels obliged to
repeat his question ("Ich darf Euch traun. Doch
sagt mir, was Ihr brütet?", 1179). Now comes the
crucial part of the evidence. For a second time
Buttler refuses to answer Octavio's question.
Buttler, who later accuses Octavio of complicity
in the deed, does not dare on this earlier occasion to inform him of his intention, because he
knows that he would prevent him from carrying it
out. "The deed will teach you", he tells Octavio
("Die Tat wirds lehren", 1180), before adding
"Don't ask me any more" ("Fragt mich jetzt nicht
weiter", ibid). The rest of Buttler's reply is
simply an assurance that he will no longer be on
Wallenstein's side. "Trust me! You can! By God!
You are not leaving him to his good angel!"

By no stretch of the imagination can it be
maintained that Buttler's reference to his not
being Wallenstein's good angel, is an indication
of his intention of assassinating him. There are
several other less extreme ways in which he can
demonstrate his defection from Wallenstein. As
we have already seen, Wallenstein's attempt to
retain the allegiance of the Pappenheim regiment
is ruined by Buttler when he announces that the
imperial eagle is being replaced by the insignia
of Wallenstein. We might add that when Wallenstein on this occasion refers to Buttler as his
"evil spirit" –
Ihr seid mein böser Dämon, warum mußtet Ihrs
In ihrem Beisein melden! (2003f.)
– this itself might be regarded as indicating
the kind of action which Octavio might well consider that Buttler refers to when he declares
that he will not be Wallenstein's good angel.

In view of the evidence provided in this
scene (W.T.2.6.), it is clear that the assertion
that Octavio gives permission to Buttler to assassinate Wallenstein is not only untrue, but
actually absurd; for if as we have seen, Buttler
refuses to divulge his intentions to Octavio,

and if the latter has no knowledge of his plan
to carry out the assassination, then he cannot
possibly have given him permission to kill Wallenstein.

Again, all the evidence in Act 5 of W.T.,
after the assassination has taken place, goes to
show that Buttler alone is responsible for it,
and that Octavio is in no way implicated. When
Octavio in W.T.5.11. challenges Buttler with the
question,"Was this the intention, Buttler, when
we parted?" (W.T.3782) –
War dies die Meinung, Buttler, als wir schieden?
– he receives no direct reply, no assertion by
Buttler that it was in fact agreed between them
that Wallenstein should be assassinated. What
Buttler does is to fall back on the fact that
the Emperor has outlawed Wallenstein, and to
claim that he has simply carried out the Emper-
or's sentence (W.T.3790).
Ich hab des Kaisers Urteil nur vollstreckt.
Just as in the earlier scene (W.T.2.6.) Buttler
did not dare to inform Octavio of his intention
of.killing Wallenstein, so now he is unable to
meet Octavio's challenge. Octavio stands justified by his honourable motive in bringing Wal-
lanstein's regiments back to their allegiance to
the Emperor, and by his innocence of any complicity in Buttler's crime: Buttler stands condemned, not only by his atrocious deed, but also
by his despicable attempt to smear Octavio with
his own guilt. The lying accusation that he un-
scrupulously flings at Octavio, that he has connived at the deed –
                Eure Hand ist rein.Ihr habt
Die meinige dazu gebraucht. (WT.3785f.)
– a charge that is repeated when he claims that
Octavio "sharpened the arrow" which he fired –
                Ihr habt den Pfeil geschärft,
Ich hab ihn abgedrückt... (WT.3805f.)
– are the acts of a man who thinks nothing of
shuffling off his own guilt onto an innocent man

whose open challenge he cannot meet. Octavio, in
declaring his innocence of the monstrous deed –
Ich bin an dieser ungeheuren Tat
Nicht schuldig. (W.T.3784f.)
– is supported by the evidence of the text; and
Buttler by his mendacious recriminations dis-
credits no one but himself. When Buttler asks
Octavio whether he has any other job for him to
do("Habt Ihr sonst einen Auftrag mir zu geben?",
W.T.3810), it has been suggested that this demonstrates that the murder of Wallenstein was a
commission entrusted by Octavio to Buttler in
W.T.2.6. There are three answers to this suggestion. Firstly, in what court of law is a mere
insinuation accepted as a proof? Secondly, the
suggestion is refuted by the evidence contained
in the text of W.T.2.6. Thirdly, Buttler's question is just an insolent rejoinder with which
he rejects Octavio's reproaches,a rejoinder com-
parable to the piece of insolence that he serves
up to Octavio in the earlier scene, when he at
first rejects the latter's suggestion that he
should come over to the imperial side. "Have you
any other orders for me?" he asks (W.T.1093).
Befehlt Ihr sonst noch etwas, Generalleutnant?
       To crown his record of infamy, this "mon-
ster", as Gordon truly describes Buttler ("Un-
mensch",W.T.3725), this insensitive "rock", this
human being who is scarcely possessed of human
feeling (W.T.2911f.) –
O einen Felsen streb ich zu bewegen!
Ihr seid von Menschen menschlich nicht gezeugt.
– has the effrontery to claim that he has "done
a good deed" by freeing the Empire of a fearful
enemy, a deed for which he claims his reward.
Ich habe eine gute Tat getan,
Ich hab das Reich von einem furchtbarn Feinde
Befreit, und mache Anspruch auf Belohnung.3801.
Only by overlooking the hypocrisy of this remark, and by ignoring the baseness of his motives, could we for a moment bring ourselves to

think of Buttler as representative of the majority of the officers and men who defect from Wallenstein. More representative are the men of the
Pappenheim regiment,inspired as they are by loyalty to the Emperor. By way of contrast, Buttler
illustrates the melancholy truth that in an imperfect world materialistic and even base motives not infrequently muddy the waters of pure
idealism.

The brutal assassination being prepared for
Wallenstein increases the sympathy which we feel
for him. On moral considerations we continue to
condemn him for his treachery, but now that he
is a doomed man and the forces of retribution
are closing in around him, we feel fear and sympathy on his account, emotions which are heightened by the irony employed. He boasts to Gordon
of his undiminished strength and vigour, even
speaking as though Fate were still on his side
(W.T.3570). Buttler has already spoken to Gordon
about his plans for keeping his commander imprisoned in the fortress at Eger, when Wallenstein pontificates in vague Biblical terms about
the "fullness of the times", when the high will
fall, and the low will be raised up, and a "new
order" will be introduced (W.T.2604ff.)
                    Die Erfüllung
    Der Zeiten ist gekommen, Bürgermeister.
    Die Hohen werden fallen und die Niedrigen
    Erheben sich - Behaltets aber bei Euch!
    Die spanische Doppelherrschaft neiget sich
    Zu ihrem Ende, eine neue Ordnung
    Der Dinge führt sich ein...
Buttler's awareness of a wave of enthusiasm for
Wallenstein among the people, enthusiasm which
causes them to think of him as a Prince of Peace
and the founder of a new golden age (W.T.3217f),
only has the effect of urging Buttler on in his
preparations for the assassination.

    Yet those references to a "new order", al-
though they contain a suggestion which comes too

late and in view of Wallenstein's moral failure
must be regarded as illusory, at least serve to
make us think of what might have been. In these
last two Acts we see, not only how impossible it
is for him, in his present position, to play
such a part, but also what great potentiality he
had in his earlier days to take upon himself the
mantle of an idealistic leader of men. But the
attempt would have had to be made, not in the
anti-moralistic spirit of those existentialist
critics who on somewhat flimsy grounds commend
Wallenstein as a prophet of a "new life", but on
the contrary after something in the nature of a
religious conversion. What chance is there of
such a moral renewal in him?

Gordon, who knew Wallenstein in his earlier
days, helps us to see him as he might have de-
veloped. It is his more complete knowledge of
Wallenstein that enables him to appeal so elo-
quently, though unsuccessfully, to Buttler, to
consider not only Wallenstein's faults, but also
his good qualities, his greatness, his kindness
and his noble deeds (W.T.2863ff.).

If there is one circumstance which softens
Wallenstein's heart, it is the death of Max, which
as we have seen demonstrates the strength of his
idealism, and his independence of Wallenstein.
The latter, who once spoke of the difficulty of
preserving one's purity in the world (WT.793ff),
has to admit that Max died without a stain on
his character (W.T.3423-5).

> ...sein Leben
> Liegt faltenlos und leuchtend ausgebreitet,
> Kein dunkler Flecken blieb darin zurück...

Indeed Wallenstein feels not only grief, but also
a certain responsibility, and even guilt; for it
was his own act of treachery which led to the
death of Max while he was leading his men back
to the Emperor (W.T.3589f.).

> Denn mir fiel
> Der liebste Freund, und fiel durch meine Schuld.

The love he feels for Max (he refers to "das geliebte reine Haupt") supersedes his customary
obsession with the power-struggle, and he again
expresses his sense of guilt by saying that it
is he who should have been the target of the
lightning that has struck down Max (WT.3594ff.).
   ...abgeleitet ist
Auf das geliebte reine Haupt der Blitz,
Der mich zerschmetternd sollte niederschlagen.
When Gordon attempts to move his heart, appealing to him to "make good his mistake", to "re-
pent" and to "return" to his loyalty to the Emp-
eror, Wallenstein as a result of his grief over
the death of his friend, is already inclined in
that direction (W.T.3644ff.).
Erfahren soll er, was ein Heldenhaufe
Vermag, beseelt von einem Heldenführer,
Dems Ernst ist, seinen Fehler gut zu machen,
Das wird den Kaiser rühren und versöhnen,
Denn gern zur Milde wendet sich sein Herz,
Und Friedland, der bereuend wiederkehrt,
Wird höher stehn in seines Kaisers Gnade,
Als je der Niegefallne hat gestanden.
In both Wallenstein and the Emperor it would be
a case of the supersession of the power-struggle
by a movement of the "heart" which would lead to
Wallenstein's repentance and the willingness of
the Emperor to forgive. In discussing this passage critics usually confine themselves to men-
tioning the negative aspect of Wallenstein's reply: blood has flowed, the Emperor could never
forgive him, and in any case Wallenstein could
never bring himself to accept forgiveness.
   But Schiller is also concerned to show how
close Wallenstein comes to a reconciliation. He
admits that if he had previously known that his
betrayal of the Emperor would cost him his dearest friend, he might have changed his mind.
Hätt ich vorher gewußt, was nun geschehn,
Daß es den liebsten Freund mir würde kosten,
Und hätte mir das Herz wie jetzt gesprochen -

Kann sein, ich hätte mich bedacht - kann sein
Auch nicht. (W.T.3657ff.)
The significance of his admission that his heart
is now urging him in the direction of repentance
and reconciliation, lies in the inference that
as a result of the sublime death of Max, the
things for which he stood - idealism, love, loyalty, humanity - all but triumph in Wallenstein
over his involvement in the power-struggle.

Certain commentators speak of Max as "opting
out of life". If he had wished merely to opt out
of life, he could simply have jumped into the
Berounka.When he seeks Thekla's advice,she tells
him to "do his duty", which as she knows is what
he has always been inclined to do. He therefore
sets off to demonstrate his loyalty by leading
his regiment back to the Emperor; and when, in
the course of that mission, he encounters the
Swedish forces, he attacks them as the enemies
of the Emperor, and so dies. It is scarcely an
adequate account of his death merely to say that
he opts out of life.

Although Max supports the Emperor against
Wallenstein, because the former has greater moral justification than Wallenstein, nevertheless
he is well aware that every champion of idealism, no matter how sincere he may be, is obliged
in opposing materialism to adopt the methods of
materialism. This is not a condemnation of idealism, as some existentialist critics seem to
suppose, but a reflection on materialism. Therefore Max, in supporting the imperial cause, has
serious misgivings concerning the methods adopted by the imperialists, particularly his father
Octavio.Quite distinct from the idealism that
employs the methods of materialism, is the pure
idealism, the moralism, the conscience and the
"heart" which is opposed, not just to materialism per se, but also to materialism employed in
the service of idealism. It is this pure idealism that is represented by Max.

The anti-idealist commentator fails to take account of the dilemma in which the idealist finds himself, confronted as he is by a materialistic world. One idealistic character, who decides to oppose the materialism of the world, finds that he can do so only by adopting the world's materialistic methods, and thus he runs the risk of being corrupted by materialism. A second idealistic character, intent on preserving his idealism in its purity, withdraws from the world.

In discussing the first type of idealistic character, the anti-idealist commentator fails to distinguish between an idealist like Octavio, who is obliged to have recourse to materialistic methods, and on the other hand a materialist per se, such as Wallenstein. As a result the commentator fails to give Octavio credit for opposing the world's materialism. In discussing the second type of idealistic character, the anti-idealistic commentator condemns Max for withdrawing from the materialistic world, or as he puts it for "opting out of life", and fails to give him credit for his pure idealism. But is it not clear that Schiller, in these two characters, represents the only two alternatives that are open to the idealist in his relations with the world, and that it is thoroughly inconsistent at one and the same time to condemn Octavio for catching the contagion of the world's materialism, and to condemn Max for avoiding the same contagion? This inconsistency serves to compound the basic perversity of the anti-idealist in preferring the materialistic Wallenstein to either type of idealist.

We must not fail to understand the significance of the death of Max, which is quite distinct from that of Wallenstein. Although Thekla cries out against the "harsh and unfeeling" Fate which causes Max to be trampled by the hooves of the horses that ride over him –

- Da kommt das Schicksal - Roh und kalt
Faßt es des Freundes zärtliche Gestalt
Und wirft ihn unter den Hufschlag seiner Pferde-
- she is by no means at a loss to understand the
significance of the tragic event, as she shows
by the following comment.
- Das ist das Los des Schönen auf der Erde!
                    (W.T.3177ff.)
Wallenstein is struck down by Fate for seeking
to rise too high in the power-struggle: Max is
struck down by Fate for opposing the power-pro-
cess with his own idealism, his moral beauty,for
it is to such beauty that Thekla refers when she
laments the tragic lot that befalls whatever is
beautiful on earth. Do not let us overlook the
significance of the contrast between the death
which Wallenstein in W.T.3.18. foresees as over-
taking Max, and the death which actually befalls
him. Wallenstein, it will be remembered, says
that Max is so closely involved in his life,
that if his planet goes off course and crashes
into a neighbouring world, setting it on fire,
Max cannot choose whether he will follow ("Du
kannst nicht wählen, ob du folgen willst", W.T.
2189), but is ineluctably doomed to suffer the
same fate as Wallenstein; in other words in the
circumstances described he would die as a passive victim of the power-struggle. But in the event Wallenstein is proved to be wrong. Max does
in fact "choose", he does dissociate himself
from Wallenstein, and his death actually represents a repudiation of the power-struggle, an
act of defiance directed against materialism.In-
deed Max,far from remaining bound to Wallenstein
by the force of his personality, demonstrates by
his death the strength of his own independent
idealism.

   The attempt made by certain commentators to
represent the imperialist opponents of Wallenstein as discredited at the end of the play, is
on a par with the shameful pretence that Octavio

is implicated in the assassination of Wallenstein. The unexpected conferring upon Octavio of
the title of Prince is no indication that in
serving the Emperor he has been motivated by a
desire for personal gain. One might with greater
justification maintain that his refusal to be
influenced by Wallenstein's offer of two Princi-
palities (P.2378f.) is proof of his disinteres-
ted loyalty to the Emperor(WW.1961.29;1980.216).
The fact that Max reproaches Octavio for seeking
to profit from Wallenstein's fall (W.T.1210) is
sometimes mentioned, but not the regret that he
almost immediately expresses at having harboured
such a suspicion (W.T.1212f.). The attempt to
pin certain descriptions on Octavio - "falsche
Katze", "Schleicher", "Schlange" - as though
they were objective statements of the truth, becomes ludicrous as soon as the reader realises
that these descriptions emanate from Illo and
Terzky, whose judgement of Octavio is about as
reliable as a report written by a gang of crim-
inals on the police who have been engaged in
tracking them down.

In the last few moments of the play Octavio
speaks in a spirit of reconciliation and comp-
assion. The distress that he shows on account of
the death of his son (W.T.3826) reminds us of
the affection he has shown for Max throughout
the play, affection which is demonstrated by his
action in leaving him with regiments who can be
relied on to remain faithful to him (WT.1266).

It is false to represent the action of the
Emperor's party against Wallenstein as a struggle against "daemonic greatness" (K.M.165). When
critics speak of Wallenstein's "greatness", do
they mean anything more than his ambition, combined with military genius which, far from serving a noble purpose, ministers only to his desire for power? What we deplore at the end of
the play is not simply the departure of such
greatness from the world (K.M.168), but firstly

the fact that Wallenstein's greatness has been debased and made to serve an ignoble end, and secondly that his leaning towards repentance comes too late.

NA. - Schillers Werke. Nationalausgabe. Weimar.
L.   - Wallensteins Lager
P.   - Die Piccolomini
W.T.- Wallensteins Tod
Jonas - Fritz Jonas,ed., Schillers Briefe
A.J.W.M. - Works of Schiller, Vol.1.trans.by
      A.J.W.Morrison, Bohn, London, 1846
J.B. - Jeffrey Barnouw, "Das Problem der Aktion
      und 'Wallenstein'", J.d.d.S., 1972
C.H. - Clemens Heselhaus, "Wallensteinisches
      Welttheater", H. & K.
H.H. - Horst Hartmann,"Wallensteins subjektive
      Schuld und objektive Tragik", H. & K.
K.H. - Käte Hamburger, "Schiller und Sartre. Ein
      Versuch zum Idealismus-Problem
      Schillers", J.d.d.S., 1959
H.&K.- "Schillers Wallenstein", ed.Fritz Heuer
      & Werner Keller, Darmstadt, 1977
H.K. - Herbert Kraft (editor), "Wilhelm Tell",
      Quellen, Dokumente, Rezensionen,
      Rowohlt. 1967
J.L. - John Locke,Vol.1, "An Essay concerning
      Human Understanding", ed.Alexander
      Campbell Fraser, Oxford.1894
K.M. - Kurt May, "Friedrich Schiller: Idee und
      Wirklichkeit im Drama".Göttingen.1948.
W.F.M.- W.F.Mainland, "Schiller & the Changing
      Past", 1957
H.R. - Hartmut Reinhardt, "Schillers 'Wallen-
      stein' und Aristoteles",J.d.d.S.,1976
W.W.(1961) - Wolfgang Wittkowski,"Octavio Picco-
      lomini, Zur Schaffensweise des 'Wallen-
      stein'-Dichters", J.d.d.S., 1961
W.W.(1980) - "Theodizee oder Nemesistragödie?
      Schillers 'Wallenstein' zwischen Hegel
      und politischer Ethik",J.d.F.D.H.1980
Théatre - Sartre,"Théatre",Gallimard,1947
E.H. - "L'Existentialisme est un humanisme",
      Les Éditions Nagel, 1967
C.L. - "Les Chemins de la Liberté",Gallimard.

INDEX